The San Francisco Fair
Treasure Island • 1939–1940

This photograph, taken from a tower of the Bay Bridge, is by Gabriel Moulin Studios, official photographers of the Fair. At bottom the causeway from Yerba Buena Island sweeps down to the southwest corner of Treasure Island, and leads past the ferry boat slips at left to the vast parking lot along the north side. At center the Tower of the Sun forms the axis of two enormous promenades. The semi-circular Administration Building and the two huge hangars to the right, built by the WPA as part of the projected San Francisco International Airport, are the only buildings surviving today. The Administration Building houses Navy headquarters and the Treasure Island Museum. (Courtesy of Tom Moulin and Moulin Studios)

The San Francisco Fair
Treasure Island • 1939–1940

Edited by
Patricia F. Carpenter
& Paul Totah

Scottwall Associates
San Francisco, California
1989

To Sarah, George, and Mildred
who took us to the Fair

All color photographs in this book,
unless otherwise credited,
are by Karl Jacob, 1906-1971.

Front cover: The Tower of the Sun, Photograph by Karl Jacob
Book Design: James Heig
Typography: Paul Totah, Michael Romo, and
Alphabetics, San Francisco

First Edition
Copyright © 1989
Scottwall Associates
95 Scott Street
San Francisco, California 94117
Telephone (415) 861-1956

Printed in Japan.

ISBN 0-942087-02-X

Acknowledgements

The preparation of this book required generosity on the part of many. In particular we wish to thank Dolores Jacob, who allowed us to use the slides of the Fair taken by her late husband, Karl Jacob. These slides were the impetus for the book.

We are deeply grateful to all of the people who so generously shared their memories with us.

We wish also to thank Lyle Bramson for helping us locate former employees of the GGIE, many of whom we have interviewed; Bertal Valley for his particular help in securing an interview for us with Dudley Carter; Peggy Brennan, Alfred J. Cleary, Jr., Serge Lauper, Sister M. Estelle, S.M., and many others who lent us pamphlets, newspapers, and magazine articles; Gladys Hansen, archivist for the City of San Francisco, for help and encouragement; and Kathryn Carpenter Totah, the link between the authors, who assisted in many ways.

Our principle sources were Eugene Neuhaus, *The Art of Treasure Island* (Berkeley: University of California Press, 1939); Jack James and Earle Weller, *Treasure Island: The Magic City* (San Francisco: Pisani Printing and Publishing Company, 1941); Richard Reinhardt, *Treasure Island 1939-1940: San Francisco's Exposition Years* (Mill Valley, California: Squarebooks, Inc., 1978); *Official Guide Book*, Revised Edition (San Francisco: The Crocker Company, 1939); and the *Official Guide Book 1940* (San Francisco: The Crocker Company, 1940).

All color photographs, unless otherwise labeled, are the work of Karl Jacob.

Preface

It would have been hard to choose a more inauspicious year than 1939 for the opening of an International Exposition whose purpose was to promote peace and brotherhood among nations. Peace and brotherhood were the most fragile of human hopes in that year. Spain had been torn apart by a tragic civil war, after which Generalissimo Francisco Franco had seized power with the aid of Fascist Germany and Italy. Benito Mussolini's troops had marched through Ethiopia, killing thousands in a brutal show of strength. Adolf Hitler and Josef Stalin had agreed not to prevent each other from grabbing Poland, Latvia, Lithuania, and Estonia. Hitler, having united Austria and Germany, was poised to roll into Czechoslovakia. Japan had occupied the coastal cities of China and was moving inland. It was already clear that Japan intended to expand her power in the Pacific.

And on February 18, 1939, San Francisco opened the gates to the Golden Gate International Exposition on Treasure Island, a 400-acre man-made wonder dredged up from the bottom of San Francisco Bay. People in the Bay Area called the Exposition "The Fair" or "Treasure Island." The rest of America called it "The San Francisco Fair" to distinguish it from the New York Fair held simultaneously. Nobody called it by its official name.

The Fair was to be an echo of the 1915 Panama-Pacific Exposition built in the Marina District to prove that San Francisco had bounced back from the 1906 earthquake and fire as a world-class, electric city. The planners of the 1939 Fair wanted to show that San Francisco not only had survived the Depression but ended up with two new wonders of the world, the Golden Gate Bridge and the San Francisco-Oakland Bay Bridge, which opened the city to the north and east in ways that went beyond mere physical connection. San Francisco could now picture itself, like New York, as a gateway to the nations that lay across an entire ocean.

The purpose of the Fair, of course, was to promote peace and brotherhood and international co-operation. The planners hoped it would also bring millions of visitors to San Francisco, with plenty of cash. But for the three million people who eventually rang themselves in at the huge National Cash Register counter at the Fair's entrance, the Fair was a chance, in the words of a popular song, to "Forget your troubles, come on, get happy."

In the years before the Fair opened, the Great Depression had brought the nation to its knees. San Franciscans, though, were lucky. They had the business from their harbor and port. They had a thriving printing and publishing industry. The construction of the bridges had brought millions of dollars (and thousands of people) to the city. Still, many of the people we interviewed for this book remember feeling the sting of hard times. They lined their shoes with cardboard when the soles wore through. They took any job, and were glad to get work, no matter how boring or menial. Labor unrest on the waterfront, which had threatened to tear the city apart, was still fresh in people's minds. William Saroyan's famous short story, "The Daring Young Man on the Flying Trapeze," depicts a young writer in San Francisco who is literally down to his last penny; his final act before he dies is to read the words on the coin: "In God We Trust."

In 1938 jobs were still hard to come by. So as the date for the Fair drew near there was a scramble for some 6,000 jobs as designers, carpenters, painters, plumbers, gardeners, waitresses, guards, guides, barkers, rolling chairboys, carnies, cops, firemen, accountants, models, swimmers, and dancers. The horticultural work alone was staggering. One thousand two hundred people planted 4,000 trees, many of them full-grown specimens uprooted from San Francisco and the Peninsula, and coaxed some two million flowering plants to grow in the salty soil.

The official theme of the Fair, Pacific Unity, was reflected in the architectural styles and colors drawn from all four continents whose shores touch the Pacific. These styles, freely adapted and generously flavored with Art Deco and other tastes of the decade, resulted in a Fair that was madly eclectic, from Bauhaus to Balinese, from Mayan to Romanesque. Fountains and sculpture, bas-relief, murals, reflecting pools, courtyards and vistas, all were lavishly combined and splendidly floodlit in brilliant, changing color. Added to these were a sod-roof Norwegian farmhouse, a Maori dwelling from New Zealand, a composite California mission, and the unclassifiable hodgepodge of the Gayway. And the focus of it all was the 400-foot-high Tower of the Sun, the slender symbol of the Fair itself.

The fifty people we interviewed for this book, with the exception of one architectural historian too young to have been at the Fair, remember it all vividly and fondly. Many of them worked at the Fair; others visited it dozens even hundreds of times over two summers. They range in age now from 56 to 97, in their experiences from the ordinary to the extraordinary. Their stories create a remarkably clear picture of the late 1930s. In the midst of all the fun and excitement, the beautiful fantasy of the Fair, harsh realities did sometimes intrude.

George Jue, at the age of 31, built and managed the Chinese Village at the request of the Chinese government, which was busy defending itself against Japanese invaders. He personally canvassed Chinese-Americans to raise money for the exhibit and supervised its construction near the Japanese Pavilion, one of the most lavish at the Fair.

Dorothy Takata, a dancer, was courted from the audience by her fiance; after Pearl Harbor, they were interned with their baby in an Arizona concentration camp.

Lyle Bramson remembers the teenage Jewish refugees whom he put to work counting ticket stubs. Marjorie Blair speaks of a German woman she befriended at the Fair who was suddenly deported. Marshall Dill, Jr., recalls that the French living in the Bay Area managed to keep the sleek French exhibit open during 1940, after France had fallen to Hitler. Norway and Estonia had to close their exhibits after their countries were overrun. And shortly after the Fair turned off its lights for the last time, the Navy took over Treasure Island and made it headquarters of the Pacific Fleet.

Yet other people said they never thought about the war in Europe. Europe for them was very far away, very remote, the countries like pieces of a jigsaw puzzle constantly being recut and refitted.

For those who went to the Fair time after time, it became a symbolic city of hope, an Oz below the rainbow, a display of what the present, not the future, already held, and a hammered-and-nailed-together definition of the American Dream where technology could make life easier, where people of all nations could live in peace, and where jobs were plentiful and paid an honest wage.

That's how most people who went to the Fair remember it. That's why most people who went to the Fair miss it. This book is a tribute not only to them but to their vision, their hope, their sense that something good lay in store for them, despite the war which was coming closer every day.

Patricia F. Carpenter
Paul Totah
San Francisco, 1989

Herb Caen at the Fair

Herb Caen, while a young columnist for the San Francisco Chronicle, *not only visited the Fair, he also took an active role. Once, for instance, he played the part of General George Armstrong Custer in the Cavalcade of the Golden West.*

On September 24, 1940, less than a week before the Fair closed, the American Society of Composers, Authors, and Publishers held a Music Festival featuring such stars as Judy Garland and Irving Berlin. Herb Caen's review of the ASCAP show for the Chronicle is reprinted here with his permission.

Fifteen thousand San Franciscans jammed the Fair's Coliseum Tuesday night to see the greatest show of its kind ever staged in this country. The Nation's most brilliant song writers, performing together for the first and probably the last time in history, staged a cavalcade of their hits — three hours of America's music. It was sensational. Showmen called it the finest spectacle of the history of American show business. It had everything — the nostalgia of the Gay 90s, the throb of Tin Pan Alley, the modern tempo of Hollywood's sound stages — but, even more than that, it had mass appeal. It was the music of the people, the American people, and spontaneously the 15,000 raised their voices again and again to sing along with the men who have given them the music they understand, that is their own and nobody else's.

The show was stopped again and again. Judy Garland sang "Over the Rainbow" and the rafters rang. The great and colorful Joseph Howard warbled his "I Wonder Who's Kissing Her Now" and the mob exulted. Tony Martin sang Jerome Kern's "All the Things You Are," with Mr. Kern at the piano, and the roof fell in. John Charles Thomas was never greater than when he performed Albert Hay Malotte's "The Lord's Prayer," and when George M. Cohan did his stuff, it seemed that no higher peak of enthusiasm could be attained.

Only one number remained on the program, and the audience seemed enervated. To present that number, a meek, quiet little guy walked to the center of the stage. Gene Buck, the master of ceremonies, called him "the nearest thing to a genius we have in this country." He didn't look like a genius. Just a dark, plain man. His name is Irving Berlin. He started to sing his song, "God Bless America." And a strange and wonderful thing happened.

Without prompting, with an indescribable feeling of quiet power and emotion, the 15,000 slowly rose to their feet. Mr. Berlin continued to sing "God Bless America." Hundreds started to sing with him. Then thousands. And when he came to the end of his song, 15,000 Americans were on their feet singing with him. Then it was all over.

Mr. Berlin walked backstage and Morton Downey said to him: "Irving, if you should die tonight, if you should wind up in the poorhouse, if anything should happen to you — you've been repaid. Just now, you've received more than any man in the world could receive." Mr. Berlin nodded. He didn't say anything. He didn't have to. There was nothing to say that 15,000 people hadn't already said.

The death of Treasure Island this Sunday night will be a sad event in itself, but the Fair's radio department has cooked up a little fillip that will probably make you bust right out crying. A few minutes before midnight, Carrie Jacobs Bond will play her "End of a Perfect Day" on a piano in the Isle's radio studios, while a chorus and orchestra accompany. As all this goes on, the lights of Treasure Island, which are being equipped with special dimmers, will slowly, ever so slowly, start to fade until only the street lamps and the Tower of the Sun remain aglow. The Tower will glisten all night until the sun rises, the poetic idea being that it never became dark. I can't decide whether this is apropos of the momentous occasion, or just plain corny.

Table of Contents

ZOE DELL LANTIS NUTTER

I was born in Yamhill, Oregon, in 1915 and moved to San Francisco when I was 17. I had taken ballet lessons in Medford and wanted to be in the San Francisco Ballet Company. When I got down to San Francisco I got a job in a nightclub and told them I was 18. It was the Depression, so you took anything you could get. I did get into the San Francisco Ballet Company and was with them for about eight years. Ballet didn't pay very much, so I continued working at nightclubs and theaters and did some modeling. Because of my ballet background I would get good jobs in the clubs as a specialty dancer. The ballet took a dim view of nightclub work, but I did it anyhow.

When I heard girls were wanted to publicize the upcoming Fair, I applied. Clyde Vandeburg, the Fair's promoter, was the man who hired me. My other boss was Ted Huggins, Standard Oil's public relations genius. They started us working as early as 1937 and dressed us in pirate suits, which seemed a natural theme for a fair on Treasure Island. The publicity men

Zoe Dell Lantis Nutter became the world's most photo-graphed woman of 1939-1940 while promoting the Fair around the country as the official Theme Girl.

would get a pirate girl booked anywhere where there was a festival or a fair, anyplace where there would be talk about the Treasure Island Fair.

My first job was at Angel's Camp, California, at the Jumping Frog Contest. Someone wanted the pirate girls to pick up the frogs and most wouldn't do it. God, I had had frogs as pets when I was a little girl, so I held them to my face. A picture of that just went everywhere. So the next time there was a place to go I was invited and my job sort of developed. I would ride horses, do anything to capture people's attention. I became known as the Pirate Theme Girl, and then after the Fair opened I was the official hostess.

The publicity people had wild ideas of what to do to capture interest in the Fair. I would do anything they asked. They had to get someone who was willing to fly around the country and who would feel comfort-

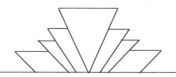

able in public in a short costume. My mother was horrified; she didn't like flying, and she didn't like the short costumes — but I did it anyhow. In Oregon, I had grown up climbing trees, riding horses and roping calves because there was nothing else to do. My father had a mill, and I used to play in the mill pond jumping from log to log. Later I did the same thing in high heels to publicize the Fair.

I was on the road more than at the Fair because we had to develop an audience. I traveled two years before the Fair opened and the two years during the Fair. We didn't have television, so we had to go out to the people. I attended the Azalea Festival in South Carolina and the Apple Festival in Washington — you can't believe some of the festivals. I made speeches at lunches and dinners and was photographed with dignitaries or national monuments, whichever a particular part of the country was noted for.

Carl Wallen had been a photographer for the Hearst newspapers and he was good. He was my boss and lined up everything for me to do. He knew how to do publicity stunts and exactly which papers to contact. We worked well together. It was really through him that we got all the attention. We'd get invited to different places, and he'd get these wild ideas. I'd try anything he asked me to do. I made a seven foot jump from one cliff to another over the Grand Canyon with 900 feet below me. I did it in high heels because they made my legs look better. I remember saying, "Oh, Carl, I don't know if I want to do this or not." He said, "You do it. You won't fall, I promise. I'll catch you with the camera." I did it about seven times; people kept wanting to see me do it.

Rarely did I see a picture I liked. I always thought I looked terrible. Most people are like that. I guess it made me keep working, trying harder all the time. Carl told me once over 300,000 copies of pictures he had taken of me were published. I was the most photographed girl during 1939 and 1940. That picture of me with the frogs got the biggest response; it went all over the world.

Colored photography was very new at the time. In

They had to get someone who was willing to fly around the country and feel comfortable in a short costume.

fact, I had one of the first colored shots in the paper ever done. It was in the *New York Daily News* and I still have it. It was absolutely earthshaking to have colored pictures in the paper.

Carl and I would often go alone on trips, and sometimes Ted Huggins or Clyde Vandeburg would come with us. I was a very lucky girl to work with such nice people. They were the only lifelong friends I made at the Fair. Carl was wonderful, Clyde was a gentleman, and Ted was one of the smartest, best men I have ever known. I was just lucky. Sometimes you can get in that business and it isn't nice, believe me.

I knew my job was special, and I loved it. Carl would say, "Tomorrow we're going to New York" and off we'd go. We'd be away two or three weeks at a time. We'd go to an air show and come back; we'd go to a festival and come back. The longest trip we took was to the Southwest. Santa Fe Railroad wanted publicity to get people to use the Santa Fe Chief and go to Indian country and the Grand Canyon. After we photographed the Indian dancers Carl wanted me to do something for them, so I did some flips. We traded that way back and forth. I ran and did a flip in the air and landed in a backbend on one foot, and they said, "She's got no bones in there," and felt my legs and back. Then one fellow tried to do the same thing and threw himself right on his head on the ground. I thought it was going to kill him, but he just got up and shook himself off. When I left there one of the Indians brought me an envelope full of Mexican jumping beans for a present. Julian and Maria Martinez gave me a little pot they had made, and I still have it.

Once I was set to open the circus at Madison Square Garden, riding an elephant, sitting on its trunk. When the elephant got ready to make its entrance it decided it didn't like me. It screamed, trumpeted, rolled me up in its trunk, and reared. It threw me out on the floor and I rolled out of the way as it came after me. The circus people then put me in a basket with Frank Buck, the naturalist who supplied wild animals to the circus, and we opened the show like that. It was scary. I had never before been on an

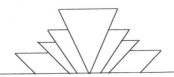

elephant, and I tell you when one rolls you up in its trunk and screams, it is something you'll never forget.

I rode horses in rodeos. I would start out with my horse, and the cowboys would chase me and pick me from one horse to the other. Whoever had me last won the race. That was called the "Sweetheart Race." Once when I started out my foot slipped through the stirrup and I kept hitting the horse as hard as I could to get it going until I got my foot free. Then I slowed down a little so one of the cowboys could catch me. If one of them had grabbed me while my foot was caught, I would have left my leg behind.

We visited every state, every governor, and every mayor of every major city to try to get exhibits for the Fair. We were successful and had exhibits from nearly every state. I stayed at governors' mansions several times. We visited Washington and invited the President. I remember Texas most. Texas is a state of mind; it has always been wonderful. Texas had the youngest governor; he was in his thirties. The South was gracious. But one state invited us not to come — Florida. The chambers of commerce of California and Florida had a big rivalry.

I went to New York to the World's Fair there. The idea of the fairs on both coasts was to develop an interest in travel. The Fair paid my salary and the airlines paid my transportation. When we went to New York I was going to invite Mayor La Guardia to our Fair, but he didn't want to see me because I had on a short costume. We got a lot of publicity out of that. *Life* magazine did two pages on it. That really launched the Fair.

Yes, I loved the job, but it certainly wasn't easy. It was supposed to look like glamour. I'd almost freeze to death sometimes. In sleet and snow I never wore a coat. I'd go skiing in shorts and do all the snow things in the pirate outfit. I was an entertainer, but it was business. I promised, took an oath, that I'd never get sick. I wouldn't dare drink or smoke. If there was a party, I would leave early; the work was just too hard and I'd get awfully tired. I didn't get many days off, but I did have one wonderful week of vacation when Mr.

> *We visited every state, every governor, and every mayor of every major city to try to get exhibits for the Fair.*

Hearst invited me to his castle in San Simeon.

I've always loved to fly. Carl hated it. He had crashed once and was in the hospital for a long time afterwards. He always got airsick. While he was getting himself together after a flight, I would stand in the door of the airplane and tell everyone how wonderful it was to fly. Hostesses had to be nurses because almost everybody got sick. Aircraft couldn't fly above the weather then so we would fly in it and would have to land often because of the weather or for fuel.

I loved the airlines because they would feed you and that was the only time I had to relax. I remember wanting to see the Mississippi River and asking the hostesses to wake me up when we were crossing it, but I was always too tired to look. I crossed the country ten times before I saw it.

United Airlines had the first non-stop flight from San Francisco to Seattle and Carl sent me on that. I think it was the 55th anniversary of the Chamber of Commerce of Seattle, and during the lunch someone said, "You're next, Miss Lantis." I said, "Next for what?" He said, "Your speech." I had never given a speech before in my life. Well, I got up there and just started talking. I told them I had lived in Seattle as a child, and although I left when I was eight or nine, I had kept up with the publicity. I said I knew it was the playground of the West and hoped they would come to the Fair. After that I got invitations to every Chamber of Commerce. That's the last time, though, that I ever ate at a luncheon. I've been afraid from then on that I'd have to give a speech. I've almost starved to death going to banquets and luncheons.

When I wasn't on the road, I was at the Fair. My job was to go around to all the exhibits and to pay attention to everyone working there. After encouraging people to come, you certainly had to make them feel welcome once they were there. I still have a fan — it is on the wall of my bedroom — given to me by the Japanese exhibitors at the Fair. I would go there and have tea and visit with them.

My other jobs included greeting arriving dignitaries and being their hostess, introducing governors

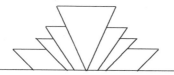

and royalty on the radio, and acting as an emcee. I presented Benny Goodman, the Dorseys and others on their shows. I danced a lot in shows there myself, which I liked. I still dance for fun now in the kitchen.

I knew Sally Rand. Smart. She had a mind like a steel trap, but was a very nice person. I did a lot of publicity pictures with her and with everyone who had a spot at the Fair.

Fairs aren't designed to make money; they are designed to draw interest to your area. Public funds are available for fairs and it's a good way to get towns rebuilt. The Fair was the nicest thing that could have happened to the whole San Francisco area.

The Fair's first year wasn't successful. Mr. Cutler, the president, was steeped in his way of doing things and liked art shows, flower shows, Souza-like music, silk hats and striped trousers. The de Young Museum and Mr. Hearst lent their paintings and Edmund Goldman's brass band was featured. It was too artistic — the highest form of art and the worst form of entertainment. That kind of amusement was going by the wayside. Young people wanted to go out and have a good time.

The second year was fabulous. Marshall Dill, the president the second year, was much more with the times and knew what needed to be done. Dr. Charles Strub, the head of the Santa Anita race track, was hired, and he had pizzazz. The big bands, the Folies Bergère and Billy Rose's Aquacade were brought in and saved the Fair.

The war changed things rapidly. At the Fair we had a Lithuanian, an Estonian, and a Latvian exhibit and I became close friends with some of the kids who ran the exhibits. In '39 when the war broke out, I was doing a show in Oregon and was gone only a few days. When I got back my friends were gone and nobody

> *It was too artistic — the highest form of art and the worst form of entertainment.*

knew where they went. I never heard from them again.

After the Fair closed, I was on the road a couple of years and then got married. Things became so critical I didn't give the Fair a thought again until after the war was over. I wanted to join the USO, but after back surgery I couldn't dance anymore. I learned to fly and was to join the Women's Air Corps, but the program was cancelled. I became a pilot and met my present husband, B.J. Nutter, when I went to Ohio to pick up a plane. He designed airplane engines and was the president of Elano Corporation. I never got tired of traveling and was a company pilot for my husband for 15 years.

I became interested in politics because of meeting governors during the Fair. In 1960 and 1964 I would have run for the Assembly if they hadn't gotten a good man to run. My husband and I are active political contributors — anyone who is good deserves support.

Being the "Theme Girl" has almost been a lifetime career. It enabled me to have contacts all over the world, and it was a fantastic education. It was a wonderful way to make a living.

The Fair was a development ahead of its time. They had colored lights, colored photography, aviation, the atom smasher from Berkeley, and the first microwave ovens and televisions. I've seen a lot of World's Fairs. I'm invited to every one as an official visitor, and I'd say ours was one of the most wonderful I could ever imagine. Ours was beautiful because of the architecture, the Pageant of the Pacific theme, the flowers and the lights. Most fairs are a twenty-first-century type of thing — futuristic. There is nothing wrong with them, but this one could be at any time, any age, and it would still be appropriate. You'd feel just as excited over it today as we did then. It was a classic, timeless fair.

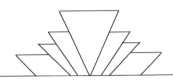

MARJORIE BLAIR

Marjorie Blair has had a varied career working with politicians, reporters, lawyers, and public relations experts.

I was 28 in 1938 when I first came to the Bay Area from Utah. I had been in San Francisco on a vacation, and I met a wealthy family who took me in tow and treated me royally. I just had a marvelous time. I went home, quit my job, and picked up my two-year-old daughter and came back.

On New Year's Eve I went out on a blind date, and the fellow I was with asked me what I was doing in San Francisco. I told him I wanted to work at the Fair when it opened, and he said, "Here's my card; go over to Bush Street and meet Alice Tapley, head of personnel. Tell her I sent you." I did as he suggested and was immediately hired to help coordinate plans for the State, City, and County Days. At first I was working for a most inefficient man, and when he and the whole staff were fired, Ted Huggins took over. I knew who Mr. Huggins was, but hadn't had the pleasure of meeting him. When he called me into his office, I thought that I was going to be dismissed. I said, "I'm a pretty good secretary. I'd like to stay along on this." And he said, "I wouldn't waste you on a typewriter." That's my first memory of him.

Ted Huggins was top public relations man for Standard Oil, and he was the one who started the Fair. Let me read from his notes: "March 1st, 1933 — As speaker at Piedmont Business Men's Club I suggested the completion of the Golden Gate and Bay Bridges be celebrated by a World's Fair in 1937. The idea was enthusiastically received, especially that part of the proposal which called for the Exposition site to be in the East Bay hilltops."

It was really his constant driving that brought the Fair about. It was kind of tough going financially, when he started in '33 to talk about having something in '37. Of course, it didn't come about until 1939; it took time to develop something as big as that. Standard Oil was behind him because they wanted to sell gasoline to bring people to the Fair. It was easier for him

5

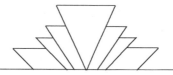

because of the people he knew and the respect those people had for him. Phil Patchin, one of the vice-presidents of Standard Oil at that time, and Howard Freeman of the *San Francisco Chronicle* were both tremendously helpful, working closely with Mr. Huggins to see that his dream became a reality.

Benny Reyes, one of the best promoters you ever heard of, was working down on Bush Street with us. We were having a hard time getting publicity before the Fair opened, and a man came down one day and said, "I'm a real horseman, and I've got a beautiful horse. I can rope anything, and I'd like to be at the Fair." There were no pedestrians or horses allowed on the bridge, of course, but Benny said, "OK, I'll tell you what to do. Get on your horse and ride over the bridge to Treasure Island. This will be a gag. The police will try to stop you. Don't let them do it. Use your rope and lasso them." The man got on the bridge with his horse thinking he was going to get a job. Of course, he was arrested, and his horse was impounded. There was a little shack which newsmen used in Marin, a hide-out place with no phone and no street address. Benny headed for the shack and didn't show up for days. I guess the man got out of jail somehow, but nobody had enough money to pay him. But we made the papers!

My job in the Special Events Department was to line up days for the states, counties and cities that wanted to participate in the Fair. People would come from various areas and be very excited about arrangements they would like to have made. We had all kinds of individual departments under Special Events. If a band was coming from a high school, for example, the musicians' union demanded that even the high school bands have clearance to perform on the Island. Our music department had to go to the secretary of Local 6 and get the band cleared. One time they didn't do it. Kids came with their instruments from one of our neighboring towns, and they were all dressed up and ready to march around the Island. They hadn't been cleared by the union, so they could just parade holding up their instruments and look as courageous as they could. They had practiced for months, but they couldn't play. So you see how important it was to be

> *The police will try to stop you. Don't let them do it. Use your rope and lasso them.*

sure that these departments were carrying through on their parts. Sometimes we had many different events in one day, and sometimes something would go wrong with every one of them.

At the Cavalcade there was a stagecoach which played a very dramatic part. The state, county or city guests would usually be interested in riding on top of that stage coach in the performance. We'd try to arrange it, one guest for each of the shows. Then friends of the lucky rider would want to see the Cavalcade, so we'd get them in, and then later take them to the Folies or to the Gayway. I felt responsible for them after we had worked together from the time they first asked to have their day at the Fair. Lots of times they would stay over on the Island until midnight, and I'd get the last boat back to the ferry building, and then get on the streetcar. I'd sit on a little seat near the conductor and say, "Wake me up when we get to 29th Avenue" — I would sleep all the way.

For a little extra token of good will, we sometimes allowed the mayor, or whomever, to turn on the lights of the Exposition. We had a little stand with a phony switch down underneath. We knew what time the sun would set and we synchronized our watches with the people in the powerhouse who really did turn on the lights. Then our visitors would flip the switch, and if we were off a second or two, you would see them standing around practically going crazy trying to figure out what they'd done wrong. To think that somebody from one little town in Idaho, or Oregon, or California had been given the honor to turn on the lights at the Exposition! It was a great experience for them, and when the timing was off, it was very shocking for them.

It was marvelous to work on that Island. One could walk down through the Court of the Moon at night toward the statue of Pacifica and think, "This is the loveliest it's ever been." It would be just beautifully planted. The next day the gardeners might have changed it completely, making it even more beautiful. The smart people from Golden Gate Park really knew what they were doing.

The thing about the Fair I enjoyed the very most was the ASCAP show where the leading composers of

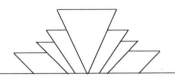

the entire country played and sang their own compositions. To hear Irving Berlin lead a group of 40,000 singing "God Bless America" was an exciting experience, partly because he couldn't sing. You know, he was practically tone deaf, but, God, he wrote some beautiful music! William Charles Handy was there, the beautiful black trumpet player who was blind, and he had his old beat-up brass trumpet and played his "St. Louis Blues."

Often I would meet a German girl on the ferry in the mornings. She told me she had come from Germany on a ship on which an Italian Vice-Consul was also travelling. There was some trouble about her being there, and the Vice-Consul put the Italian flag around her luggage and kind of took care of her until they docked in New York. She was beautiful, but she had an aura about her as if something were wrong. One day we met for

> *To hear Irving Berlin lead a group of 40,000 singing "God Bless America" was an exciting experience partly because he couldn't sing.*

lunch and she said, "I'm awfully glad that we got together today because I won't be seeing you again. I'm being deported." It was shocking; I couldn't even ask why. She said she was going back to Germany, and I should look her up in the phone book if I ever got to Germany. 1939 was an interesting time.

Working at the Fair was a sentimental experience, and I don't mean just what happened to me. Aside from the romances and marriages, people made very dear friendships over there. It was a simple time in many ways. We had our favorite newspapers and we believed, to a great degree, what the papers told us. We didn't have a half dozen different commentators, a half dozen experts analyzing everything for us. Maybe its better this way; I don't know. But I'll tell you, I really liked that naive, sweet time. I was happier then.

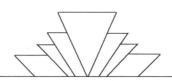

JERRY BUNDSEN

The Fair came at a needed time. It's hard to put it this way, but it was like nothing was happening. Nothing much going on. Nothing to occupy your mind. There was no place to have fun. I was a young public relations guy at the time.

One of my clients at the Fair was Sally Rand. I handled her publicity. I'd get her interviews on the radio, get her, if I could, to a ribbon-cutting ceremony. There was a lot more newsprint available in those days because of the four San Francisco papers, two in Oakland, and one in Berkeley. It was just a case of getting her name in the columns. You had to think up items, you know.

Sally got her start, I think, at the Chicago Fair. She came out to become a partner at the Music Box in San Francisco and she put on some great shows there. For instance, the Ritz Brothers. You want to talk about being funny? I don't think there's anyone around today that could top the Ritz Brothers.

Everyone remembers Sally Rand's Nude Ranch at the Fair. She herself was all business. She had her girls all decked out with western outfits without tops and with skimpy bottoms. Sally would get up on the balcony where the patrons couldn't see her or hear her and she'd yell to the girls: " Come on Nadine. Get over there and jump more, will you? And Helen, for God's sake, get up off your duff and walk over and bend down to pick the basketballs up." She used to stand up there like a maestro running an orchestra.

One of my favorite stories about Sally was something that happened shortly after I was married. My wife was with me one day when I went to see Sally on business. We were waiting by her dressing room and she opened the door and came out flat ass naked and said, "Come on in Jerry. I want to talk to you about those ads." My wife almost fell over. After I came out of the dressing room I had to convince her it was like being in the bedroom with your Aunt Emma getting

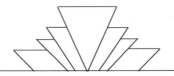

dressed, or something. You never paid attention to her at all.

At that time I also worked as Herb Caen's assistant. He had just come down from Sacramento two or three years before to write a radio column. Then the newspapers, in their great wisdom, decided they weren't going to give free publicity to a competing advertising medium so they killed radio columns. Takes a lot of brains to do that. So Herb didn't have a job, in effect, and he suggested to the publisher that he write a "Round-the-town" column. They didn't know if it would go. I remember when Herb told Bill Saroyan about the possible column, Bill said, "You're going to write about San Francisco every day?" Herb said, "Well, I'll give it a try."

I had been dealing with Herb Caen because I handled publicity for the agency that handled CBS in town, and I had to go to see him all the time for publicity, that kind of stuff. It was our mutual love for Benny Goodman that brought us together, though. We used to go out on the beach in Herb's old Plymouth on Tuesday nights when Benny was on "The Camel Caravan." We'd get an It's It, the candy bar thing, and sit out on the beach, looking at the water and listening to Benny Goodman on the car radio. That was the big highlight of the evening.

We were like two stardust kids when Benny came to Sacramento to play a one nighter. I told my boss I wanted to bring the columnist from the *Chronicle* to get a column out of it. He said, "Well, hell, go if you can." So Herb and I jumped in his Plymouth, drove to Sacramento, and called Benny on the house phone of the Senator Hotel. Benny said, "Hey, come on up. Let's have dinner." God, Herb and I were going to have dinner with Benny Goodman! Of course, we got to be friends, from then on, until he passed away.

When Benny was hired to play the second year of the Fair I handled his publicity. It was just wonderful having that band play at the Fair. You couldn't move in the crowd when they played. It was the big thing. You just never lived unless you stood in front of that band with people really dancing. I mean the jitterbug. You could really dance in those days when you listened to that beep. Those guys were just giants. They didn't have to have all that amplification, you know with the fire and smoke and lights flashing. I try to tell my grandson who's 21 what it was like then. It was

Elvis Presley and Sinatra rolled into one.

Of course the Fair had the usual exhibits. A good friend of mine named Sam Levine ran a Gayway show, but I forget what it was. I know he lost his shirt on it because he spent all his money inside, installing nice seats and everything. You can't do that in a carny atmosphere.

There were other things that were interesting. For example, the big extravaganza, "The Cavalcade of the Pacific." They used to do "Custer's Last Stand" as part of the show. As a matter of fact, one night Herb Caen played General Custer and I was his Indian assistant. We went over and they got buckskins for us. The director told us when the Indians rode by and started shooting, we were all to die and leave Custer to the last. After we died the announcer came on to talk about Custer's last stand and the guys rode by like mad on horses. We sure had a hell of a good time with that.

One of the shows of that Fair was called "Birth of a Baby." It was a movie. As my wife, Norma, who was 17 at the time, and I walked by, the guy putting it on, Breckinridge, called out, "Jerry, be my guest. Go on in." Before the film started a guy comes on and announces if anyone gets faint, there's a doctor right there. So this thing comes on. If I remember right it was in black and white and it was like a medical film, the birth of a baby. I looked over at my wife and she was white in the face. I had to carry her out and they gave her smelling salts in the other room. When she felt well enough to leave, Breckinridge was standing there, and he said, "Hey, I'm glad to see you enjoyed the show."

My wife was a model then, and she worked at the Fair in the Westinghouse exhibit. That's where they had the first robot — one that could talk. She was also the model for the China Clipper. We have several pictures of her on that thing. Do you realize it had a dining room? When it took off, everyone wondered if it would make it. It followed the shipping lines, you know, just in case.

My wife and I lived right on Telegraph Hill and we looked right down at the Fair. If you didn't see it then, you can't know what a glorious sight that was with those golden lights out in the Bay. It was just wonderful, and the ferries, of course, going across every 15 minutes. Beautiful!

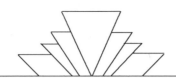

PATRICIA LILEY

I remember going to a class reunion, Burlingame High School it was, and everybody asking each other how things were going. "Oh, just fine," I said. "My company came through the crash beautifully. No sweat at all." I was working for The Hartford Insurance Company and had been there since I left the school. Well, it wasn't a month later that my boss called me in and said, "Miss Chase, we won't be needing your services as of the first of next month."

That night I went to a company Halloween party. I was literally dancing with tears in my eyes. I was smiling, but not inside. From that time on I did temporary work, office jobs. The Depression had hit.

One day I was walking down Market Street and lo and behold there was something going on at a theater there. I stuck my nose in. I have an awful dose of curiosity. I learned it was Sally Rand recruiting people for the Fair. Being interested in show business I got in on the interview.

I eventually worked at three different places at

Patricia Liley donned a costume at Sally Rand's Nude Ranch and acted as an extra at the Cavalcade. She lives now in San Jose.

the Fair. I appeared on the stage at the Calvacade. I just had to mill around in the mob scenes dressed in a pioneer outfit. Then on the Gayway there was one exhibit with a picture of a nude called "Gloria." It wasn't "Stella," but it was something similar, a beautiful young woman lying out on a couch. I stood out in front with the barker. He would give a big spiel and handcuff me and then show the mystery of it, how I could break out of the handcuffs. It really was nothing complicated. I just turned my hands and the cuffs came off. The idea was to catch people's attention so they would buy a ticket to go in to see the picture.

I was also in Sally Rand's Nude Ranch. The girls wore bandanas which were full around the chest area and two guns in holsters, one in front and one in back in strategic places, Stetson hats and boots.   There were mules which we could ride, or we could play bad-

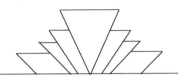

minton, walk around the porch of the Ranch House, whatever we wanted as long as we kept moving. The customers walked past on the other side of a glass wall. Families went by, not just men.

The Nude Ranch was supposed to be risque. Sometimes we would be raided. The police would come roaring up and everybody on the whole Island would come rushing over to see what was going on. The police would close the place down, and it would be in the papers that Sally was busted. The next morning it was business as usual. In fact, more business than usual. Whenever business started slacking down there would be another big raid. It was always a blaring of trumpets.

I got to know some of the people from Ripley's Believe-It-Or-Not. Sometimes after taking the last ferry home at night we would go to Foster's on Jones Street and have something to eat and chitchat. There

> *Whenever business started slacking down there would be another big raid. It was always a blaring of trumpets.*

was the man with the rubber arms. He was quite tall, and he would put his arm out and extend it another foot. I don't know how he did that. Then there was the girl who had no arms and did everything with her feet. She would play instruments and write with her toes. She was a lovely little thing. The girls at Sally's were nice, but I really didn't get to be friends with any of them.

One night I was sitting at the Fair having my dinner, and I started thinking about an old friend. The sun was going down, a beautiful sunset it was, and I don't know what struck me, but I decided to write him a letter. We had met about ten years earlier when he was living in St. Helena. We dated quite a bit, and then just drifted apart. I hadn't heard from him in quite a few years, but he answered my letter. Lo and behold, he came down to see me and popped the question. I was in the mood, so I left the Fair and got married.

MARSHALL DILL, JR.

The World's Fair idea started in 1852 with the famous Crystal Palace in London which was the brainchild of Queen Victoria's husband, the Prince Consort Albert. It was an attempt to demonstrate technological progress not only of Great Britain but of all the countries that exhibited there. Then Napoleon III had two world's fairs in Paris during his reign in 1855 and 1867, again centering around technology. These years marked the beginning of the development of steam power, cast iron and steel. To a certain extent the fairs exemplified national boastfulness of the countries that were invited to take part and an effort to spur trade and international commerce. The artistic and amusement aspects were distinctly sideshows. Vienna had a fair in the 1870s; Paris has had one approximately every 10 years, one in 1878 to show that it had recovered from the Franco-Prussian War, and one in 1887, whose monument is the Eiffel Tower.

Our fair in 1915 was an attempt to show the world that San Francisco had recovered from the earth-

Marshall Dill, Jr., son of Marshall Dill, who served as President of the Fair during its second year, lives now in the Marina district, retired after many years of teaching.

quake and fire. It used the symbol of the Phoenix rising from the ashes. Another theme was the opening of the Panama Canal, symbolized by a giant pushing apart two huge cliffs. We had the Fair on Treasure Island in 1939 to celebrate the two bridges which had opened within six months of each other.

I don't know that fairs evoke strong memories any more. Fairs held in recent years seem to have been both artistic disappointments and financial disasters. My mother and father used to speak about the Panama Pacific International Exposition as such a happy period, so gorgeously beautiful. Mother and Dad were married in 1914 and that fair was in 1915.

My father was in business in San Francisco long before the Fair opened. He worked as an importer-exporter and also as a sales agent. He was always very civic minded. He had a love affair with San Francisco

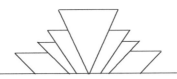

his entire life. As far as he was concerned, any other city was definitely fourth-rate compared to San Francisco.

From his early days he associated himself with the San Francisco Chamber of Commerce. He was chairman of the Foreign Trade Committee in the days of World War I. Dad was the president of the Bohemian Club in the middle thirties and was elected president of the Chamber of Commerce in 1939. The usual thing was to re-elect the president for another year. In the Fall of 1939 a group, including Mr. Dan London of the St. Francis Hotel and Mr. George Smith of the Mark Hopkins and representatives of the Palace and Fairmont, who all stood to lose a great deal if the Fair didn't run for a second year, came to Dad and asked him if he would relinquish the opportunity to be president of the Chamber and instead take over the job of opening the Fair for its second year. He accepted that offer.

There was some doubt about opening the Fair for a second year. It was in very bad financial shape, as was the simultaneous New York Fair. Dad's job was to retrieve as much money as possible. I think the Fair was finally able to pay off more cents on the dollar than would have been the case if it had stopped after the first year. The second season was shorter. It was perhaps a mistake to open the Fair the first year in February. Despite all our boasts about California weather, February can be mighty cold and windy. Even though there were wind protection devices, it could be very chilly over there.

The second year opened in May. Before that Dad and my stepmother were invited to the opening of the New York Fair. I was in Cambridge then doing graduate work, and I came down to New York to spend the weekend with them and went on the opening day. New York, too had serious financial difficulties, so the leaders tried to make the show folksy the second year. Their slogan was, "Hi, Elmer." On the opening day people ran around with badges on their chests that said, "Hi, Elmer." The Fair was supposed to appeal to the grass roots level and to avoid the silk hat. Dad ordered a silk hat from Brooks Brothers to be waiting for him at the hotel. When he arrived at New York he

All went well until I felt a little furry creature pushing around my shins and ankles.

found he wasn't to wear it. He brought it home and wore it here. San Francisco is always a little more dressy than New York. I remember the president of the New York Fair and Dad chatting and, as I recall, Dad said, "I'll see you next week when you come to our opening." He did come to the opening. So there was not competition, but cooperation between the two.

Dad had an office on the Island which is now the museum. That building was to become the headquarters of Pan American Airlines. Dad's office was in the center of the second floor. There was a bedroom and a bath in case he wanted to take a nap or change his clothes. Every morning he was presented with a list of the affairs that were to occur that day. If he had to have a change of clothes, he would telephone my stepmother to bring over the suit he needed that afternoon and tell her how she should be dressed. Marian, my stepmother, loved those activities. She had a grand time at the Fair.

The first year of the Fair I was here all summer and decided I was going to see all the exhibits. I went every day for a week and visited every exhibit. I talked into a telephone and heard my recorded voice; that was pretty exciting. There were all kinds of gimmicks there. I visited all the foreign exhibits, too. The Australian one was particularly pleasant because Australia has some of the most exotic animals in the world. There was a tiny zoo outside the building.

One day I had "exhibition feet." I had walked for hours so I went to the Australia building because I knew they had a movie. I thought I could take my shoes off in the dark and no one would notice me. All went well until I felt a little furry creature pushing around my shins and ankles. A wombat, a tame wombat, was allowed to circulate among the guests. It had decided that my warm feet were a cozy place to stay for a while.

In 1940 the Fair lasted until October. I went to a number of the parties and occasionally met some of the distinguished guests. My most vivid memory is Women's Day at the Women's Club House which is now the Officers' Club. The Women's Club House was run by a group of San Francisco women, headed by

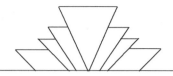

Mrs. George Cameron, whose husband was the publisher of the *Chronicle*. Her maiden name was Helen de Young, and she had spent summers in Meadowlands in San Rafael, her father's home. It is now a residence at Dominican College. Mrs. Cameron and her committee organized a day to celebrate distinguished California women. This was long before women's lib. The format was so set that twelve or fourteen distinguished women were chosen to be honored but none of them were allowed to say a word publicly. To each of them was assigned a man, presumably a good friend, who spoke for them. They stood up, took a bow and received much applause, but they could not say anything. That was *strengst verboten*. Among them were two famous novelists, Gertrude Atherton and Kathleen Norris, and also my aunt, Maude Fay Symington, who had been a famous opera singer in Germany. I knew Mrs. Atherton, so I was picked to introduce her. I had a great teenage crush on this very distinguished old lady. She was a wonderful woman, a delightful conversationalist, and a fine writer.

Kathleen Norris was introduced by her brother, Joseph Thompson, a great wit in his own right. Mrs. Norris may not have been a great author, but she was one of the wittiest and most delightful women that God ever created. I remember one little story about her: I went to her fortieth wedding anniversary. She and Charles Norris, also a novelist, and some of their friends started a little musical program. Uda Waldrop was at the piano, and distinguished MacKenzie Gordon was singing. Then someone unplugged the lamp over the piano. George Creel, the federal representative at the Fair and a close friend of the Norrises, saw the plug and leaned over to replace it. Kathleen said, "Thank you Creel; that will be all. You may go now." It was that kind of quick remark that was a constant delight.

I remember going to a luncheon at the Women's Club given for Lauritz Melchior, the great Wagnerian tenor. He was an enormous man as wide as he was tall. I was six feet tall but I was like a pygmy next to him. He had chosen to marry one of the smallest women I have ever met. She was very petite, very cute; they made an amusing pair. Another night Bruno Walter conducted the San Francisco Symphony in an all-Wagner program. Oddly enough, Kirsten Flagstad was in the audience but did not sing. Dad couldn't come to the Island that night. There was going to be

a reception in the Pacific House and he asked me if I would identify myself to Madame Flagstad, then and now my vocal goddess. He asked me to offer his apologies. Nothing could have pleased me more. Flagstad was dining with a very close friend of hers and ours, Mrs. Milton H. Esberg. Madame Flagstad had perhaps the greatest voice in the world but she was a rather awkward personality. She smiled, but I was disappointed.

Special days were held for celebrities at the Fair. Two such days were held for Governor Thomas Edison of New Jersey, the son of the great inventor, and Wendell Willkie. Willkie had a great day at the Fair because there was a presidential election that year and he was the Republican candidate. Dad and a good many of the leaders of the Fair were businessmen, all Republicans, so they gave Willkie a "bang-up" day. Willkie was handsome with an infectious smile. I have a picture of him sitting atop his car waving to the crowd with his wife, my father and stepmother also in the car.

Mr. Thomas Watson, who for many years was President of International Business Machines, had an IBM day at the Fair. That was the splashiest occasion of the summer because Mr. Watson brought out a special train of employees from IBM, a very patriarchic institution. Lawrence Tibbitt, the great California baritone, and Grace Moore, one of the outstanding opera stars of the time, and others, gave a wonderful show in front of the Federal Building. Thousands of people came to hear them. Dad said that if there were any chance of financial difficulties, he could always suggest a second IBM day because more people came to the Fair on that day than perhaps on any other.

All did not go well on Treasure Island. A fire completely gutted the California Building. The decision was made not to do anything about it because it occurred so far into the season that the expense of rebuilding it would not have been recoverable.

Sally Rand's Nude Ranch was very tame compared to anything you can see on Columbus Avenue and Broadway these days. There's a picture in my photo album of Dad standing with Sally Rand with a big pair of scissors in his hand, cutting the ribbon that officially opened the Gayway, the amusement area. It would not be called the Gayway if the Fair were given this year.

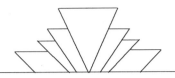

M A R S H A L L   D I L L ,   J R.

Pacific House was one memorable spot on the Island. It was headed by Mrs. William Denman, wife of a federal circuit judge. She came of an old San Francisco family; her maiden name was Leslie Van Ness. Van Ness Avenue was named after her father, a former mayor of San Francisco. Mrs. Denman was very civic-minded. She was particularly interested in the Indians of the Southwest. She used to go there and study their culture, especially their dances. Pacific House was devoted, as the name suggests, to the countries of the Pacific Rim. It was decorated with four huge murals of different parts of the Pacific painted by the famous Mexican painter, Miguel Covarubbias.

It is curious that the two fair periods in San Francisco, 1915 and 1939 and 40, took place early in the two greatest wars history has ever known. The fairs had been planned before either of the wars broke out, but the conflicts did cast a shadow, because some European nations withdrew their participation or never had any. There was no German building, but there was an Italian one, at least during the first year. France, I recall, had a pavilion, but alas, France was overrun and defeated in May and June of 1940. So, although it was able to operate during the first year, the French building in the second year was supported by local people who wanted to keep France alive.

There was throughout the United States a great deal of effort to help the refugees from countries that had been forcibly occupied: Latvia, Lithuania, Poland, Estonia, Norway, Denmark, The Netherlands, Belgium and France. Dad tried to curtail these activites. He believed that the Fair was meant for fun. Yes, there were beautiful and serious artistic events — music, drama — but it was essentially a place where grandpa, grandma, mother and dad and the children could have a day of fun on the weekend, enjoy themselves on the rides on the Gayway and go and see the exhibits. He felt it was bad to bring in the tragedy of Belgian, Dutch and Norwegian Americans who were so terribly dismayed and unhappy about the fate of

I don't know that fairs evoke strong memories any more. Fairs held in recent years seem to have been both artistic disappointments and financial disasters.

their homelands. Thus, although there were some demonstrations of that sort, Dad tried to restrict them as much as possible. He talked to me about it one day. I thought he was wrong. I was youthfully sympathetic with the people who had been attacked and defeated by the Germans and the Soviets and the Italians. He explained his position to me, and I then understood that the Fair should be for pleasure and for happy occasions. Let the gloomy ones take place in the City but not on the Island.

The Japanese Pavilion was one of the most splendid. I have a doll, elaborately dressed with a kimono and headdress, which the leader of the Japanese mission at the Fair presented to Dad about a year before the Pearl Harbor attack.

One of the hangars built on the Island was used for one of the most superb exhibits of fine arts that has ever been in San Francisco, or indeed the United States. It included loan objects which will probably never be lent again, for example, Botticelli's "Birth of Venus." That exhibit presented a very real problem because in June 1940 Italy became a belligerent. My father, as executive of the Fair, was responsible for these masterpieces. He was very much alarmed about the insurance and safety possibilities. I don't know how it worked out, but the works of art remained in this country until well after the war. There was no question of transporting them across the ocean during wartime. The Germans would not have wanted to torpedo them, but the risk was great. They remained in the United States for a number of years—where, I don't know—and were eventually returned to the Italian government.

Treasure Island for my generation was a kind of Land of Oz, a place where many things were brought together that would never be in one place at any other time. If you were a scientist, there was much for a scientist to be interested in. If you were interested in fine arts, there were wonderful paintings and concerts. For San Franciscans old enough to remember, it was an unforgettable experience.

15

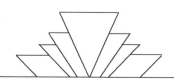

BISHOP FRANCIS QUINN

I have had several opportunities to go to world fairs. I went to the Expo in Montreal, the Fair in Brussels in 1958, the New York World's Fair, and the one in Vancouver last year because of church committee meetings that just happened to be held at world fair cities. I found the '39 Fair on Treasure Island just as enjoyable as these others. The others may have been more sophisticated with exotic media shows and that kind of thing, but for its time our Fair on the Island was dazzling.

To celebrate our graduation from high school, our whole class from the seminary went to the Fair. I remember taking a boat ride out to Treasure Island. Out of the 25 of us, six or seven got seasick. Eighteen or so of us were ordained as priests seven years later. But the joy of it then was in our youth. Sometimes today I can't understand how my grandnephews, when they go to some place like Disneyland or Marriott's Great America, aren't interested in the more educational things. They just want to take rides and listen to rock groups. But looking back on it, that's

Bishop Francis Quinn attended the Fair as a boy of 17 after graduating from the seminary. After years of ministry in San Francisco he is now Bishop of Sacramento.

exactly what interested me when I was 17.

I'm sure we were rambunctious in the 1939-40 era. I can remember doing things that young people today would be thrown in jail for. We just looked on them as pranks — like shooting out streetlights with a rifle. I thought nothing of that at Halloween time. Actually we didn't do anything too mischievous at the Fair.

That summer after our graduation, my friends and I went over to Treasure Island as many as eight or ten times. We tried to do different things each time. I guess we would have been most interested in what was known as the Gayway, the carnival part of the Fair. The thing I most remember is Sally Rand. I don't think we ever went in. In those days there was nothing very immodest about the show because everything then was much more subdued.

At the Fair my joy was that of any teenager:

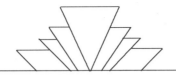

having fun, eating scones, staying up late, and staying overnight at friends' houses because I lived in Napa.

When I went to Vancouver, I was very interested in going to all the countries' exhibits. As you get older you become more interested in the more serious things. But I suspect we went through serious exhibits rather hurriedly at Treasure Island. We didn't want to stand around in one spot too long. There was so much to see. We didn't have a lot of cash in our pockets. If there was anything free around, we did it.

When at 17 you're thinking of becoming a priest, you don't have very profound thoughts. Even though I was in the seminary, I don't think at that age I was religiously oriented. I don't remember dancing at the Fair. We never were really encouraged to dance. That's a little different in seminaries today. But back then they used to tell us to guard our eyes when beautiful girls went by. So we didn't presume to dance.

I remember a display of a baseball catcher's ability. Joe Sprinz was a catcher for the San Francisco Seals and he tried to catch a baseball thrown from a blimp. It went through his mitt, and I think knocked out some of his teeth. His face is still somewhat marked by that. I was there the day it happened. While I didn't see it, I can remember the crowds gathering.

Esther Williams was the great swimming star in Billy Rose's Aquacade. We were all very much enamored of her. This was the first time I had seen celebri-

Back then they used to tell us to guard our eyes when beautiful girls went by.

ties such as Esther Williams, Benny Goodman and Johnny Weissmuller. I remember Weissmuller flailing away at the Australian Crawl, though that wasn't the way he wanted to swim. He told Billy Rose he moved faster if he swam smoothly. But Billy Rose told him if he would splash away, it would look as if he were moving faster. Isn't that a strange little footnote?

I remember listening to Benny Goodman and Ziggy Elman playing "And the Angels Sing." That was the hit at the time. I identify times by the songs that were popular.

The automobile exhibits were very interesting to me. I remember looking at 1940 Fords and Chevrolets that were selling for about $900. Young people were welcome to hop into cars. In those days there was less fear of vandalism.

I remember the Clipper planes landing. They had pontoons and it was a very slow descent. They seemed to land on water at about half the speed as on land. They kicked up a lot of water and would pull up at the port right there on Treasure Island.

I was a boy from the country. Although I was born in Los Angeles, I grew up in Napa, and then spent my high school years in the seminary on the San Francisco Peninsula. So just the splendor of all the buildings and of the scientific exhibits was very striking. It was the place to go. It was like today's malls which are the gathering places of teenagers. The Fair was just the natural place for teenagers to go.

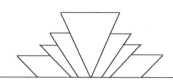

EDMUND G. "PAT" BROWN

Edmund G. "Pat" Brown, Governor of California from 1959-1967, is now a senior partner in the Los Angeles law firm, Ball, Hunt, Hart, Brown and Baerwitz.

I was ten years of age at the time of the 1915 San Francisco World's Fair. I remember it well. I climbed over a fence and didn't pay any admission fee. I came home and told my mother. She didn't think anything one way or another, but she told my father. My father made me go back and pay the admission fee, after I had sneaked in! He said, "You can't do that. You have cheated them out of 25 cents admission fee. You have to go out there and pay it." It made a deep impression on me and gave me a tremendous respect for my father.

I was not very big in 1915, and a great many of the "fun zone" places impressed me. One place in particular was an opium den, a Chinese opium den. You paid, of course, to go in to see it. It scared the life out of me. You would see the figures of the old Chinese men smoking opium. After that I never would try or even touch drugs of any kind.

I remember very well some of the entertainment at the Zone: the scenic railway and "Stella," a large painting that seemed to be alive. She was on the Gayway at the 1939 Fair, too, but didn't seem as exciting to me in 1939 as she did in 1915.

I remember the 1939 Fair shows more than the buildings of foreign countries. The Folies Bergère was great. I remember the swimming gal, Esther Williams. That was a magnificent swimming exhibition. I remember the young Art Linkletter and his interview show. It was excellent and started him on his career. He also was the spokesman for the Cavalcade — another very good show.

I remember particularly going to see the Indonesian Exhibit, which was very interesting. They had an excellent restaurant of unusual food. The life in the Far East as portrayed at the Fair was very exciting.

The Fair didn't get participation from some foreign countries because the war had started in Europe. But San Francisco went ahead with the Fair on the man-made island anyway. It was a beautiful Fair,

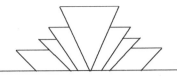

tremendous lighting and beautiful buildings.

In 1939 I was practicing law in San Francisco with the firm of Brown, McDonnell, Macken, and Brown. It was a young firm; none of us were over 35. Our firm did everything in 1939 — personal injury plaintiff cases, a large divorce practice, some bankruptcy and small corporation legal work. It was a general practice firm. We did very well.

In politics my father had been a Republican so I became a Republican when I first registered in 1926. Soon after I started practicing we had the Depression of 1929. Hoover was President from 1928-1932 and as a Republican I supported Hoover — made speeches for him all over the state. In 1932 Roosevelt was elected. I must confess that I was really dissatisfied with the policies of the Republican Party in 1932, but I campaigned for Hoover anyway.

A young man by the name of Matt Tobriner and I had both been presidents of the Debating Society at Lowell High School in the early 20s. He went on to

> *My father made me go back and pay the admission fee after I had sneaked in!*

Stanford and Harvard Law School. My father had been in the portrait photo business. He was unsuccessful and he had to close his business. I could not afford to go to college immediately, so I went to night law school at 18 years of age. Seven years later, in 1934, Matt and I both had our law offices on the same floor in the Russ Building. One day we met in the hall and he said to me, "I'm going to change my registration from Republican to Democrat." I said, "Matt, you can't do that. It's like changing your religion." He said, "Well, say you no longer believed in your religion and believed in another. Do you think you should stay in a religion that you no longer believed in?" I thought you should not, so I said, "You are right. I'm going out with you and change my registration." I've been a Democrat ever since and a very active one.

I ran for District Attorney in 1939 and was defeated. In 1943 Roger Lapham was elected mayor. The same year I was elected District Attorney. This started my political career.

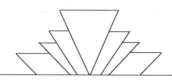

NELL FANNING

I was born here in San Francisco on Clementina Street in my grandmother's old Victorian; we didn't go to hospitals in those days. I came into this world in April, Easter Sunday, 1892.

I was raised in the Mission District right near the home of Governor Rolph. My father had a big business on the corner of Hyde and McAllister which was totally destroyed at the time of the earthquake and fire. It was made of brick and collapsed during the earthquake, and everything burned up. I was about 13 years old, and my father took my hand and said, "Come on. Let's go up on the hill and see if we can see the fire." We did, and saw our city burning. Then he took me in a horse and buggy downtown, and we had to get the militia to recover our belongings. One of the soldiers shot a gun at the cash register so it would open up. My father took out $20 gold pieces that had melted in the fire in the form of a cross, and we kept that in the family for years as a souvenir.

I can smell earthquakes coming. This is earth-

Nell Fanning, a visitor at the '39 Fair, had a preference for the 1915 Fair where she met her husband. Their daughter, Patty, met her husband at the 1939 Fair.

quake country, and I can't for the life of me figure out why they've take our Muni and lined the whole thing with brick. I am not Calamity Jane; I'm hoping we'll avoid it, but when that big earthquake comes along and all the bricks go flying — you remember what I said.

I was at the Panama Pacific International Exposition in 1915. That's where I met my husband. It was at Stow Lake in Golden Gate Park, around which I still hike now and then; I do one mile a day with my friend. My cousins took me over there one day, and we were taking pictures sitting on the rock by the water. Along came a boat — "The Nellie." One of the girls said, "Here comes your boat, Nell," so we waved at it. One of the girls had met the boy who was in it with my husband-to-be, so they pulled over to the water's edge. This boy said, "I've got some passes for the new fair that is just opening up. Let's make a date now, and I'll

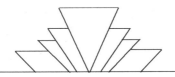

come by and pick you up." So that's how we started going together; our marriage lasted over 65 years.

My husband was in on the beginning of all the activities of San Francisco. He purchased the right-of-ways for Lombard Street and 19th Avenue. He was a civil engineer and helped design the Golden Gate Bridge. He had nothing to do with the engineers who came out from the East to actually build the thing, but we had access to it and were able to go on the bridge all the time it was being constructed. We saw it right from the bottom up. We were one of the first to ride up to the top of the towers in the freight elevator. The wind almost blew our heads off!

The Treasure Island Fair idea was born after the Depression, and World War II came right after. My husband worked in City Hall and had passes for Treasure Island and the California Building. We used the passes quite a bit.

We were able to park our car right in the center and visit a lot of places that we probably wouldn't have gotten into if we had had to pay admission.

There was one place where you could go to sample food. They'd cook all the foods of the different countries and on a cracker we'd have samples of everything. Once in a while we had cooking demonstrations. As far as sitting down at a table with a white tablecloth and beautiful glassware, there wasn't a lot of that at that Fair. We picked up sandwiches and coffee — quick meals like McDonald's today.

Artists would come in for a day or so and leave. I met Diego Rivera over there; he was a rather eccentric old man. He had young artists as his assistants who did most of the work. He came in and sort of supervised, and of course he was very bossy when he came. "I don't like that; take it down, take it down," he would say. So they would have to do the whole thing over. He was so particular about his art. He always had a lot of people in his pictures. It was at the time of Harry Bridges and his labor movement, and it was mostly labor, labor, labor you heard about. We didn't like Rivera's pictures. He used crazy colors for those days. They weren't the kind of pictures we were interested in.

We didn't like Rivera's pictures. He used crazy colors for those days.

They had the Fashion Arts Building, too. Of course, a lot of people went to the fashion shows. The clothes were more practical and not as glamorous as some of the older ones shown at the 1915 Fair.

I remember Art Linkletter put on a big show. In fact he was there quite a while—two or three months. He appeared on the stage, but his talking was so fake. He taped the show, and then he stood there on stage with his mouth open, making gestures, and trying to get the coordination just right. Sometimes the tape would go off the air just at the time he'd be saying something, and you couldn't hear anything. That's where he got his start.

One Sunday afternoon I personally met Gus Kahn, Johnny Mercer, Walt Disney, Oscar Hammerstein, Billy Rose and Irving Berlin, who were in the Fine Arts Building performing.

Most of the activities were at the California Building. Hetch Hetchy was the main thing displayed there. My husband was one of the surveyors who originally went into Hetch Hetchy Valley, and he was very much interested in its construction. So I looked at that exhibit from head to toe.

We went to the Aquacade and found it very attractive. The swimmers would form the shape of a cartwheel in the water. That's where my son and daughter learned to swim. We used to take them over there in the afternoon after school. At that time they had instructors for children.

They had the most gorgeous coloring on the buildings at night. I remember they'd have a mauve shade, and then it would change and go into apricot, and then it would it turn to blue. That's how I got the idea for decorating my living room.

We drove over to the Fair most of the time. They discouraged using the ferries because they wanted us to use the bridge. We had been used to ferries. I think I was about 11 years old the first time I went with just my sister on a ferry to Grandma's in Alameda, and we passed Goat Island, which was later called Yerba Buena. It was like Alcatraz or Angel Island; it just stuck up there and nobody bothered much with it.

I don't think the Treasure Island Fair was as nice as the first one in 1915. Of course, I was in love and had

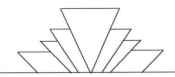

romance at that time. With the 1939 one I was married and had two high school kids. In fact, that's where my daughter, Patty, met her husband. She came home one night and said, "Mom, I met the cutest young officer, and, oh, is he darling." They've been married 45 years now, and have three grown sons and many grandchildren.

Of course, everybody was more or less worried about the war coming up. Hitler was running around creating a big disturbance, and *Il Duce* was in Italy. World War II was a pretty serious situation, and we didn't know what we were getting into at all with the blackouts and everything. At the time we were all trying to prevent war in this area because we were afraid of being bombed.

> *They had the most gorgeous coloring on the buildings at night. That's how I got the idea for decorating my living room.*

I don't think you'll find there was too much enthusiasm for this Fair because, as I say, at the time most of us were tired and worried about the war. The war dampened the spirit of the Fair, and that's why they lost money on it.

I do remember well the last night of the Fair. Oh, it was just beautiful. Luckily, we had no fog; it was just a nice clear night. Thousands and thousands of people were there that night. We stayed out until about ten o'clock, and then the lights faded and went out. It was just beautiful. When we came home, we found that our house had been robbed. We saw everything out on the floor and upside down, the mattresses off the beds and the pictures off the walls. Oh, boy, that was the finale!

Opposite: The Tower of the Sun, here seen through the Arch of the Winds, held a 44-bell carillon on which blind pianist Alec Templeton played Bach's fugues. The carillon is now in Grace Cathedral.

Above: The South Towers in the Court of the Moon were the first landmarks of the Fair for drivers coming off the Bay Bridge.
Left and opposite top: Orchid-tinted blue lights flooded the towers by night.
Opposite below: The view from the north included the Tower of the Sun.

Above: The Magic Carpet, 25 acres of multi-colored iceplant, spread out on both sides of the Elephant Towers, the main entrance to the Fair. The plants thrived in this exposed area where no other flowers could.
Left and opposite: Try to see the cubist elephants on the tops of the towers.

The Temples of the East in a Balinese style were flanked (opposite top) by dramatic gold bas reliefs depicting the "Dance of Life." Bernard Maybeck and William Merchant designed the Temples.
Opposite below: The view from Pacific House shows a glimpse of the Japanese Pavilion and the Tower of the Sun.

Overleaf: Herman Voltz designed two huge murals for the front of the Federal Building. The one shown here depicts the "Conquest of the West by Land." Artists of the Federal Art Project actually painted the murals. In front of the mural an Elephant Train stops to let sightseers take it all in.

Top: One of 16 galleon prows, tipped with the winged Spirit of Adventure, looms over the Court of the Seven Seas. Bottom: The wind baffles at the main entrance offered little protection from the icy breezes coming off the Bay. Opposite: The Arch of the Winds frames the Rainbow Girl fountain-sculpture with the Federal Building in the far background.

The four great elliptical windows of the Pacific House symbolized the four continents of the Pacific: Australia, Asia, North America, and South America. Designed by William Merchant, the building was beige in 1939 and was painted a deep brick red in 1940. Inside, a brilliantly colored glass map showing the trade routes between the continents filled the north wall. Other maps and dioramas dramatized the Pacific theme of the Exposition.

Top: Asian and European masterpieces in the Art Building outdrew the Gayway in attendance. Katherine Caldwell remembers that the chief curator spent the night in the building guarding the art objects before the Fair opened. In 1940 the exhibit changed to "Art in Action," which allowed visitors to watch Dudley Carter, Diego Rivera, Herman Voltz, and other artists in the throes of creation. Bottom: Mayor Angelo Rossi and Chief Administrator Al Cleary extended lavish hospitality from the San Francisco Building.

William Wurster designed the Yerba Buena Women's Clubhouse. It offered dining rooms, lounges, cocktail bars, a children's room, beauty shops, and "other feminine conveniences" according to the official guide book, which went on to warn, "This club house is not open to the general public." The building survived as the Officers' Club for the Navy until it was demolished in 1988.
Opposite: The Mission Trails Building displayed the chief architecutral features of the California missions. Inside, "the world's largest moving panorama, 165 feet long and 18 feet high," showed the beautiful landscape between San Francisco and Los Angeles.

The Alameda-Contra Costa Counties Building showed a diorama of the East Bay, as well as a.picture of UC Berkeley when it had a total enrollment of eight students.
Left: The White Star Tuna Building served hot tuna turnovers with frozen peas, the latest thing in fancy foods. The classic Art Deco building ended up beside Highway 101, north of San Rafael.

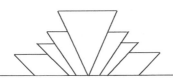

DOROTHY TAKATA

My father was a stage person. In the Orient he used to play the drums and a long flute made of bamboo. When he entertained in our community church in Alameda I would get up on the stage, too, from the time I was a little girl, and show off a bit. One day a friend said, "Come on and I will show you different kinds of dancing." I took to those lessons and I would go home after them and find some rags to put on for costumes, and I would dance and dance.

So when the Fair opened and they needed dancers I just fit in. I always danced there with a group of girls, all girls. The men did their own dances. I knew Balinese dances, Hawaiian dances, and Thai dances. But my main dancing was Japanese.

My aunt had come from Japan and had brought a beautiful kimono for me, the one I wore at the Fair. I have it yet. It is black with long, long sleeves, decorated with all kinds of colorful flowers. We didn't wear shoes when we danced, just the white tabi. We had lots of white powdery makeup on our faces and we

Dorothy Takata danced at the Fair and, soon after, was sent to an internment camp in Arizona with her husband and baby. She now lives in Oroville.

put up our hair nicely, almost like it was lacquered. In our hair we put those chopstick-like pins with silver beads or shiny flowers hanging down.

We wore different costumes for the different kinds of dancing. I used to be able to move my neck the correct way for Balinese dancing, but I can't do that any more.

We did our Japanese dancing outside the Japanese Pavilion. There was a little bridge, a reproduction of one at Kyoto, and we danced near there on a platform that extended over a pool beside the Pavilion. We danced about twice a month, sometimes for celebrities, for men who came from Japan for meetings and parties, and sometimes for the public.

Between our practices and performances we would go in a group to see the rest of the Island. What stands out in my mind are the flowers, the lovely fountains, and the fireworks. I particularly enjoyed

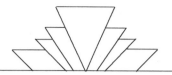

the evenings, the night time and the lights. Oh, I have never seen such beauty!

I lived in the Berkeley Hills with an English couple, the Earl Gaylords, and we had watched the construction of the Bay Bridge and Treasure Island from their living room windows. After the Fair opened, every night we would watch the fireworks. My mother had died when I was young, and the Gaylords took care of me as if I were their daughter. I lived with them from the time I was in high school until I was married.

I got married with the help of a go-between. My father and my husband-to-be's folks arranged with a go-between to find out about our histories and our horoscopes to see if we could be compatible. It was planned that at the Fair when I was dancing one day we would all meet and have tea. He was to look me over to see whether he was ready to get married or not. I was to look him over to see if I felt like being his wife. He came to watch me dance. Then at the tea we were both bashful and didn't say a word to each other. We just looked each other over to see if this was the person we would live with as husband and wife. It was a casual tea ceremony, but I was so nervous I couldn't have the tea and I couldn't eat a thing.

Afterwards the go-between contacted me. "Well, Dorothy, what do you think about this fellow? Do you think you'd like him to be your future husband?" I said that I thought him to be a nice young man. He seemed to be interested in things that I was interested in. He had gone to Waseda University outside Tokyo. He was an American citizen. He was also a fencing teacher and held the black belt. He liked the things I liked. So I said yes.

We didn't meet again before the wedding except for a picnic and the movies, which we attended with other family members. He was living in Watsonville and he would telephone. Long distance calls were expensive then but he would call and tell me when he was coming to the Fair to see me dance. I guess I was falling in love then because I would look for him in the audience. We didn't talk to each other, nothing like

> *We were like sardines in the train going to Arizona. My baby was crying, all the babies were crying.*

that, because I had to stay with the other dancers. But I would see him, and he would see me.

We were married about six months later, on December 8th in Watsonville. We had two ceremonies: one in the Oriental way and I wore a kimono, and then I changed to a traditional white gown for the second ceremony. They were both in the same Buddhist temple, the same day. That was in 1940.

Our first daughter was born in 1941, shortly before Pearl Harbor was bombed. There was quite a commotion during that time because my husband had a history of traveling to Japan. He had been educated there at the University and was in training to be a diplomat, so he was suspected in Washington of being a spy. When the war came, the FBI came and took him away. Then they sent him back and our family was sent to the concentration camp at Poston, Arizona.

We were like sardines in the train going to Arizona. My baby was crying, all the babies were crying, but we were young then and we had the strength we needed. The first year at the camp was particularly hard. Many people died, the old people because they couldn't get used to the change, the food, and the climate. There were suicides because people thought they were going to be left there to rot. My husband worked in the kitchen and he finally went to those in charge to complain about the food. When he saw that they too were eating the same thing, we all felt better. Little by little we got used to things.

The years after the war, getting our lives together again, were very hard. We were sent to Illinois, but finally returned to California. After the training my husband had had at the University, he settled for the life of a farmer and a landscape gardener. We had 43 years together before he died. He was a wonderful father to our two daughters. He was, and I am, very proud of them. And now there are two grandsons. It's a closely-knit family. I like to tell our daughters and grandsons about the tea ceremony at the Fair, the beginnings of my happy marriage with their father and grandfather.

GEORGE JUE

We started preparing for the Fair in the late part of '37. A number of community leaders came to Chinatown to look for somebody to participate, to represent China. I was then the President of the Company of Six. Japan had started a war with China on July 7 of the previous year. China was so busy they couldn't spare the time or the money to do anything cultural in this country. So they asked if any overseas Chinese would like to take over. I was willing. I had to barnstorm the country to get the money in the interest of China. We had to save face and represent our country. I went from San Francisco to New York to Boston to Chicago to New Orleans — wherever I could find money.

We had about three acres of the fairground, and we put a wall around it. The management had to approve our designs. We had an architect who was a member of the Bohemian Club to look the designs over and to put it together. The architect was able to trace the origin of buildings in China and get pictures of them. But he'd draw something and then change it; he was a perfectionist. For someone to go into business and use this fellow as an adviser would be all right. But he was too costly because he was too detailed.

I was 31 when the Fair opened and I was there every day as general manager. A lot of people came up to me and said, "Gee, what a young guy. You're so young!" Something was always happening at the exhibit so I had to be there the whole day long. I very rarely got around to the other parts of the Fair. I was very much in demand to publicize the Chinese Village, to answer questions about it. Art Linkletter once interviewed me at the St. Francis. He had that program on for a long time. He was, at the same time, in the publicity department for the Fair. He was a nice guy, very friendly.

In my talks with the staff I always pointed out that we represented China. I'd tell them, "We must

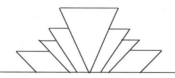
present a good show; we must represent China because China itself cannot participate. We must win friends for China. We're on a stage, and people from all over the world are coming to see us. We cannot reflect unfavorable things. So everybody on his toes. Everybody do his best." I'd tell the staff to make sure they looked neat. Lots of us dressed in Chinese clothes. I wore Chinese clothes all the time at the Fair, but I'd take them off at home and hang them in the closet.

> *We lost money — in the hundreds of thousands of dollars. That damned pagoda itself was probably at least $75,000.*

People enjoyed seeing the Chinese Village; it would touch them. They would say, "Chinese people do have something. They have years and years of culture." They saw that, for example, we'd had Chinese porcelain for years, while in America it was not common. Visitors mainly commented upon the jade exhibit. It was shown in the biggest building in the village. (That building is now in Sebastopol in Sonoma County.) There was always a line to see the jade. We used to charge 25 cents to enter that building, but if I met some distinguished guests, I would take them in the side door so they wouldn't have to wait so long. I personally escorted J. Edgar Hoover, the head of the FBI at the time. He was friendly and gracious. I opened the door for him, and he said, "Oh, thank you." He liked the exhibit and said it was worth his trip coming out West. For anybody who came to the Fair, the Chinese Village was a must.

Visitors also noted that the carvings on our buildings were beautiful. We had Chinese art and paintings, very famous, which went back hundreds of years. They are now on display in the National Museum of Taipei. I saw the exhibit recently in Taiwan. They've lost some of the things, but they have most of the better things. They didn't have room to take them all, so they took the best.

Princess Der Ling, one of the Empress Dowager's ladies-in-waiting, had her own building in our Village. We used to have a joke, that for the Empress Dowager she was mostly waiting. She had come from Peking and was living in Berkeley at that time with her husband, Mr. White. Officially she was still Princess Der Ling, but when she and her husband were at home, they were known as Mr. and Mrs. White. She was very gracious. I was also trying to be very polite to her. I had staff members who took care of whatever she needed. I didn't have much of a chance to see her socially except when she came in and went home. I'd politely say good night and good morning to her. Mr. White had worked at the American Embassy in Peking in some capacity and they met there.

Our acrobats would perform two shows in the afternoon and one in the evening. They were from Northern China, and the whole troupe was selected because of their ability. I remember the first time I watched one of them jump through a hoop of fire. I don't know how he did it, but every day he would jump through it three times and no accident ever happened. We also had girl singers who sang opera as part of the show.

I enjoy those years with fond memories, but financially we all took a beating. We lost money — in the hundreds of thousands of dollars. That damned pagoda itself was probably at least $75,000. No one works at a fair to come out with any profit. The exhibits generally just make enough to pay the working wages, to keep up the payroll. Treasure Island was like another world. If you ask me personally now what I think of it, it was good, but it was not a place to make money.

The reaction from the people to our exhibit was favorable. If it weren't for us, there would have been no representative from China at all. Japan had a big exhibit. Quite often the big subject, the daily conversation, was the war. We were sad that, for no reason at all, the Japanese invaded China. Happily there was no rivalry between our exhibits. People were not trying to outdo each other. We all tried to be gracious and friendly and to do the best we could.

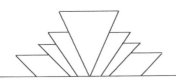

CASHEL GAFFEY

I belonged to the Choir at St. Peter's, and everyone was raving about the new cop on 24th Street. I wasn't aware of him myself until we met during a Knights of Columbus trip to Yosemite. It was the first time I went away from home without my family. The group was to meet at the Ferry Building. Ed O'Brien was there, that's Monsignor O'Brien's father, and he had a thick Irish accent. He was from County Kerry, the same as my mother. When he introduced me to Mike I thought he said "Mike Gatti." Mike was dark; he had coal black hair and heavy dark eyebrows. After he started talking I thought, "He's not Italian; he's Irish!" After the Yosemite trip I didn't see him again until the next summer when we were at Adams Springs. That's where the friendship began. We were married three years later, August 25th, 1926.

Mike was the cop on the neighborhood beat, a patrolman. By 1937 he had risen in rank to lieutenant, and in 1939 he was made Acting Chief on Treasure Island. He was in charge of all the police and auxiliary police on the Island. There was no real crime at the Fair that we ever heard about. Maybe people had to watch their wallets and purses, but that was all. There weren't even traffic problems. They had a regular police station with a holding cell, but as far as I know, no one ever had to be put in the cell.

My husband, of course, had to be there every day, and the family would go over often to see the displays and the like. I remember they brought in snow for a ski slope; that was something different for San Franciscans.

The Balinese women with their long, tapering fingers impressed me. We watched them working with inlaid silver. They were very agile, sitting cross-legged on the floor to do their work. They were graceful, too, when they danced.

Czechoslovakia had an exhibit of ladies in their native costumes, showing their crafts. We were there the day Germany invaded Czechoslovakia, and the ladies were crying in their costumes.

43

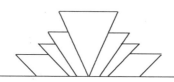

MARY HUTCHINGS

My father served as Acting Police Chief on the Island. He felt the job was glamorous because he had a chance to meet everyone. He met the Aquacade stars, Esther Williams, and Johnny Weissmuller. He loved the Cavalcade. The fact that it was outdoors made it very interesting. It was about California, the pioneers coming West, the wagons, the campfire at night. In those days we didn't see that much even in the movies, but this was actually on the stage. It was amazing. My father particularly loved a song from that show called "Cattle Call." We had that record, and we would play it over and over on a wind-up Victrola.

There was so much to see at the Fair. I remember the sumo wrestling at the Japanese Pavilion. They did a dance there, too, with flags and swords.

Mary Hutchings went to the Fair with her mother to visit her father, the Acting Police Chief on the Island. She now lives in Millbrae with her family.

I remember the Chinese Opera. I didn't understand it; the music was so completely different.

The kangaroos in the Australian exhibit put on a boxing match. They even had boxing gloves on. A mother kangaroo had a baby in its pouch and we had to wait and wait to see it, but finally it did put its little head out.

There was an exhibit in the Hall of Science on the effects of drugs. Opium, I guess it was. In that building they also had television and hydroponic gardens where they grew tomatoes and all sorts of vegetables. Remembering now what was at the Fair I can see those who were responsible for the exhibits had vision.

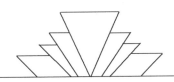

KATHERINE CALDWELL

I did my undergraduate work for two years at the University of Wisconsin, and then I transferred to Harvard (Radcliffe). When I first went there I had an entree to one of the professors in art history, Langdon Warner, a great specialist in Japanese art. He was a friend of my stepfather, and Professor Warner and I became friends as well as professor and student.

I took a course at the Fogg Museum at Harvard — the first course given in the United States in museum management. I had majored (concentrated, as they say at Harvard) in philosophy. I was married just after I graduated in 1928. My husband was finishing his Ph.D. in English Literature at Harvard, and I got a master's degree there that year in Art History. We came to Berkeley and I worked first at The Legion of Honor in San Francisco.

In those days the Bay Area was very naive about the arts, maybe not music, but certainly in the visual arts. After all, in San Francisco at that time the museums didn't really amount to much. I had been

Katherine Caldwell, many years a teacher of art history at Mills College, was the Director of Education at the Palace of Fine Arts during the Fair at Treasure Island.

"living" in the Boston Museum during my studies. It was quite a contrast. I felt a kind of pleasure in being able to share my knowledge. That was the attitude I had; maybe it was a missionary attitude.

In 1939 I was working in what's now called the Museum of Modern Art. Then it was called the San Francisco Museum of Art. A remarkable woman named Grace Morley was the first director of that museum. She had gotten her degree at the Sorbonne although she was an American. She gave complete freedom to people under her to do exactly as they wished. She put me in charge of the Education Department although I had never had any education courses. Perhaps because my parents were public speakers, it became natural to me to communicate.

My great teacher, Langdon Warner, was in the area at that time. He had a two-year leave of absence

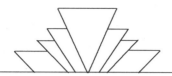

from Harvard to put together what became an extraordinary exhibition of art for the Fair at Treasure Island. He gathered art from every country whose shores touched the Pacific Ocean, although the richness and variety of the works from China and Japan made them overshadow everything else. Some were folk art pieces and some were very sophisticated — ceramics, jade, sculpture and painting.

This was the first time that a significant amount of material had been gathered in San Francisco for an Asian collection. There were some works of art from The David Collection in London that have not been inside this country before or since. It is a great collection of Chinese ceramics, chiefly Song Dynasty. But people weren't ready for it. People had no idea what they were looking at; they had nothing to pin it on, you know. You can't blame people for not appreciating something without some background and instruction. A Cambodian piece (that San Francisco could have bought for very little, but whose rarity was overlooked) was one of the most beautiful things there. It was a Buddha. That piece was greatly admired by people who didn't know a thing about Buddhism because it had a serenity about it. People could see something there, intuitively, whereas other works of art required more background knowledge.

When I was teaching at Mills College some time later, a young lady came to me one time and said, "I've lived in India. My father is in business there and all Buddhas look alike to me." And she said it just like that, in a very hostile way. "Well, my dear," I said, "you are not obliged to take the course, but if you are to take it, I hope when you finish it, all Buddhas wouldn't look alike to you." But that's typical, and understandably so, of the Western attitude. Maybe all Christ figures would look alike to somebody from a culture where the Christian story was completely unknown.

One of the beautiful buildings at Treasure Island, Pacific House, exhibited contemporary art in Asia, and Grace Morley was connected with it. It was probably she who recommended me for the position of lecturer at the Palace of Fine Arts. I was very inter-

There are so many ways of describing subtle colors in Chinese. They have names for colors such as "the sky after the rainstorm."

ested in doing this and working under my great professor once again.

To the anguish of Professor Warner, when the works of art arrived, we couldn't install them for public display because the buildings weren't finished. Since there was no bonded guard, Warner got a cot and slept there and guarded the treasures himself. He had such a great sense of responsibility. You know art people are not supposed to be as efficient as business people. We made a point that the art people had everything ready on time, but the business people had not followed through!

My official job was Director of Education for the whole Palace of Fine Arts, which was divided into both the East and the West. As you entered the building when you turned left, you turned to Asia, and when you turned right you went to Europe. The most famous European pieces of art shown were Botticelli's "The Birth of Venus" and Raphael's "Madonna of the Chair." The attendance, to be sure was very much less for Asia than for Europe. Those were the days before anyone really knew anything in any depth about Asian art. They thought of Chinatown and tourist trinkets as Chinese art. A journalist in San Francisco wrote an article which downgraded the whole Pacific Cultures show and said nobody wanted to go there. He believed that when you went into the museum, you wanted to turn to the right rather than the left. It was an unfortunate article because the thrust of the Exposition was to present Pacific cultures. It was not very helpful to suggest that this art was something to be avoided rather than sought after. If we hadn't had those famous paintings from the West, perhaps the contrast of the crowds wouldn't have been so great. If it had just been the Pacific Cultures Show, the number of art seekers would probably have been greater. And I don't think Asians attended in any great number. They have only rather recently participated in San Francisco in the support of their own culture in terms of art.

There weren't any docents at that time, and I was one lecturer for both the Asian and European sections.

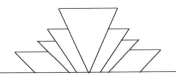

Eventually I could not handle the number of people (we had thousands), so I asked another person if he would take over the European part. One thing that was very helpful was the little lecture hall. When the crowds were very large, we would usher the visitors into the auditorium and there we could present the material in a way that everyone could see at once.

When it comes to craftsmanship, I can't imagine anything that is harder to appreciate, on first acquaintance, than Chinese ceramics of the Song Period. There are so many ways of describing subtle colors in Chinese. They have names for colors such as "the sky after the rainstorm."

I'm very partial to Chinese sculpture and to Japanese paintings. Some very great works came from Japan. We were plunged into the Second World War shortly after this Exposition. The terrible thing was that some of the people in Japan who lent their treasures were accused of being pro-American. One of them, an elderly collector of refinement, who was interested in art, not politics, was jailed for a while.

There was an entrance fee for the Palace of Fine Arts and the fact that our attendance exceeded that of

> *He gathered art from every country whose shores touched the Pacific Ocean.*

the Gayway pleased us. In the Gayway there was a woman who posed in the nude in the style of a great painting by Manet. We were struck with the fact that she was posed so much like the picture that we went to see her several times and got well acquainted.

Although she was very intelligent, she had little education and no knowledge of the painting. We showed her the picture by Manet and it was lots of fun.

I went to see the rest of the Fair, but I was working awfully hard and didn't have much time. I was a wife and a youngish mother, and I had not taken a full-time job before.

When San Francisco had the opportunity to acquire the Brundage Collection, there were still enough people who remembered the exhibit at the Fair and realized that after those pieces went back to Asia, we did not have anything that represented the arts of China and Japan that could be called museum quality. I think it opened people's eyes to the fact that we had no great museum of Asian art. I'm a devoted enthusiast of Chinese and Japanese art. I think Langdon Warner's exhibit acted as a stimulus for acquiring quality Asian art in San Francisco.

MILDRED VAN EVERY

Mildred Van Every, a social worker for many years, worked among the Indians in the Southwest and helped the Indian artists at the Fair.

The Indian exhibit at the Fair in 1939 was wonderful. Local people, Charles de Young Elkins, Judge William Denman, and Mrs. Denman, had a great deal to do with making it one of the finest exhibits. René d'Harnoncourt, who later became the director of the Museum of Modern Art in New York, was in charge of the exhibit. He and different Indians came out about seven months ahead of time to make the plans. That's what made it so good. It was sort of a coordinated thing between the Indians and the Fair officials.

About 125 Indians came, members of tribes from Alaska down to the Seminoles. Some stayed two or three weeks, and others stayed longer. Everybody thought the Indians would get awfully sick of the Fair if they had to ride street cars and buses and all, so a place on Yerba Buena Island was found where they could live while they were here to demonstrate their arts.

The Navajo men did the sand painting which they use in ceremonies of healing. They sat on the ground at the exhibit and took natural ground rock, red, blue, white, and black — the kind you can find down in canyon country like Monument Valley — and they sifted it through their hands. They made large symbolic pictures, working out the designs as they went along. Visitors sat there all day to watch.

At 4:30 they would come to the house for dinner, and after dinner I would drive them over to the exhibit. The sun must never set on a sand painting, so they would go back to blow it away. It was very serious. Religious. Totacasi, the medicine man, did a little chanting when they blew the sand.

The Navajo women are the weavers. Zonnie Lee, the famous weaver whose work is in the White House, was at the Fair, and so was her granddaughter, Dollie May Lee. Dollie May's son graduated in electrical engineering this last spring, I believe from the Univer-

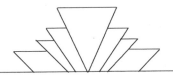

sity of Utah, so you see what vast changes have gone on.

Wood carvers from the Tlingit tribe of Alaska, Mr. Wallace and his son, carved a cane which they presented to Mrs. Roosevelt when she visited. Mr. Wallace also carved a totem pole, but I don't know what became of that.

You've heard of Maria and Julian Martinez of San Ildefonso? They are the world famous pottery makers who invented black-on-black pottery. They knew exactly what temperature and smoke make it black. Well, they were both here at the Fair and they stayed all summer making their pottery. An Indian bowl is all hand crafted. They have no wheel. If you have ever tried to work with clay, you know after two or three inches it falls apart. Well, when the Indians work with it, it doesn't fall apart. They make wonderfully thin bowls.

Geronimo Cruz Montoya was also here from Santa Fe. Now her hair is all white, but she used to have the most beautiful black braids — just like satin. Somebody in Palo Alto recently had an exhibit of her paintings. I went down, and she was there. We got to talking; we rattled on and on about the days of the Fair. It's been 50 years, but an Indian never forgets you.

We had wonderful times with the Indians during the Fair days. Mrs. Lewis Marshall Lloyd, a great friend of Indians, had a Pierce Arrow that held seven people, and nothing pleased her more than to get them in that car and go up to Mt. Diablo for a barbecue. The famous silversmith Ambrose Roan Horse used to get down on his hands and knees and do the barbecuing of the lamb. In Navajo country you want to order lamb. It's the best lamb you'll ever taste.

In the evenings at the house on Yerba Buena Island, the Indians liked to do their dances and they liked to play cards. The minute supper was over they would pull out the cards and play poker. One day I happened to be downstairs at 9:30 when they were

> *The Indians would never ride elevators, but they all got on the escalators. In fact, they didn't want to get off.*

breaking up their card game, and I noticed Julian Martinez pushed all the change into his pocket. I said, "You know, Julian, I'd hate to have Luke Big Turnip go back to North Dakota with no money from his time here. It would make me feel very bad." He said, "We wouldn't want to make you feel bad." The next night they played with a lot of chips, aluminum chips, instead of money.

We wanted the Indians to see something of this part of California while they were here, so we arranged for a trip to Yosemite for one of the outings. As we drove along, I kept saying to Willy Spanish, a Blackfoot, "Don't you think this is beautiful?" He'd say, "Yes. Very nice." Later when I went to visit him in the high Rockies in Montana, I could see why he thought our mountains were pretty tame.

The Indians used to like to go shopping in San Francisco for shawls and stockings. They had to go early in the mornings, of course, because they had to be at the Fair at 10:00. The Emporium used to open early just for us. The Indians would never ride elevators, but they all got on the escalators. In fact, they didn't want to get off. It was the funniest thing they had ever done.

Near the end of the Fair René d'Harnoncourt entertained everybody at Izzy Gomez's restaurant on Union Street in San Francisco. The tables had bowls filled with real fresh fruit because we never had liquor around, and this took the place of liquor. Dr. Alfred Kroeber, after whom Kroeber Hall at UC is named, was also at the dinner. After we had eaten, René stood up and said, "Dr. Kroeber is going to tell us a story." Everyone look up politely. Dr. Kroeber started, "One day a coyote went out for a walk..." and they simply looked at him in astonishment. The coyote is the animal god of all, the trickster. All of them, from Alaskan Indians down to the Cherokees, burst out laughing because they all knew the story. What a marvelous evening that was. It was a wonderful summer, I tell you.

DUDLEY CARTER

My family had a logging camp in the wilderness country about 60 miles from New Westminster, British Columbia, where I was born in 1891. There were just a few white families living there among the Indians. In 1906 we moved into Haida and Kwakiutl country in Northern British Columbia. My only schooling was in a little Indian school which I attended for only five months. I could learn more at home with my father who had had a very good education. But in those days it wasn't too necessary to pass education on to the children because there was no way they could use it. All we worried about was how many logs we could get in the river in a day. That was all we needed to know.

When I was six I was already doing a man's job. All day long I would run on the skid road in front of the oxen. With a bucket of crude oil and a rag at the end of a stick, I would dab the crude oil on the skids in front of the logs so the oxen could haul larger logs to the river.

Dudley Carter was a featured artist during the Exposition's Art in Action show, and now, at the age of 97, still wields his double bitted axe to carve monumental wood sculptures.

By the time I was a young man, I was a self-taught forest engineer and free lance cruiser. There were only six or eight free lance cruisers who covered the whole Pacific Coast. Our job was to explore and map the country and give an exact report to lumber companies on the nature of vast forest areas. These big timber companies needed to know the complete information on what kind of timber was in an area, and how it could be taken out. If we could come to within five or ten percent of what they actually logged we qualified as free lance cruisers and were of great service to the industry.

I would work every day alone in the wilderness for up to five and a half months at a time, running dangerous rivers, climbing precipitous mountains, and at times encountering mountain lions, bears, wolves or killer whales. The others worked in pairs, but I usually worked alone because we got paid by the

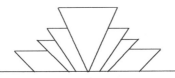

acre and I could make better time alone, and did not want to subject a partner to the hazardous chances I would take.

Living among the Northwest Indians while their culture was still active gave me the opportunity to observe the carving of the great totems, the war canoes, and the huge community houses built without nails or hardware. The work I create has grown out of this experience, born and developed on American soil without foreign influence.

In the early 1930s I started experimenting and carved "Rivalry of the Winds," a 4' x 14' sculpture representing a local Indian legend. Dr. Richard Fuller purchased the sculpture and installed it as a feature work at the Seattle Art Museum in 1932. That put me on the map as a monumental wood sculptor. The depression was a reality at that time, and I thought there would be better opportunities in San Francisco. So my wife, my daughter and I moved down there.

Evidently my reputation as an artist had gone before me because I was engaged immediately on the Federal Arts Projects. I lived in San Francisco, and later on the banks of the Carmel River, working half-time for the Federal Arts Projects and half-time for myself.

In 1935 I met Timothy Pflueger, a prominent San Francisco architect. I had entered my first large redwood sculpture, "Condor," for the opening of the new San Francisco Art Museum, and Mr. Pflueger really liked it. In 1939 he commissioned me to design and execute the facade on the Shasta Cascade Building for the Golden Gate International Exposition at Treasure Island. The work I did for that building was nearly 30 feet wide and had a height of about 34 feet. It was completely carved in low relief on top quality sugar pine. It represented the industries and wildlife of Northern California. Although the art critic for the *San Francisco Chronicle* wrote, "It cries vehemently for preservation," it must have been destroyed. I can find no trace of it. I also carved six eagles for the court of the same building, and I've found no trace of these either.

In 1940 the Exposition produced the great Art in Action show. Visitors came into a large area of the

> *At one time in Mexico City Diego Rivera had kept Trotsky in his home for several years.*

Fine Arts Building and watched artists use a variety of media. It was here that Diego Rivera painted his huge fresco mural, "Pan American Unity." This great work almost covered one wall of the interior. The opposite wall, approximately 300 feet away, was the site of a huge marble mosaic, constructed and designed by Herman Voltz. Out in the center of this vast and active area I was attacking a 30 ton redwood timber, set vertically and encircled with a skimpy version of a hand operated elevator. This sculpture, "The Goddess of the Forest," was designed to represent important principles in totem design. The head, arms, and legs were abstractly distorted to fill the circular form of the tree. Instead of removing the wood between the arms and legs, I carved into it some other forms. The characters were all interlocked one into the other, from one end to the other.

Sonja Henie, Edward G. Robinson, and Charles Laughton were among the many visitors who were interested in my work. Charles Laughton had trouble climbing to my 30-foot level to visit. My narrow passageway was not wide enough for his wider waistline.

After the Fair "The Goddess of the Forest" was donated by the G.G.I.E and myself to Golden Gate Park, but, because my request to allow air to circulate under the sculpture was disregarded, it was, in time, badly damaged. In 1984 I went to San Francisco to restore it. It was moved from the park to San Francisco City College where it is now, along with the Diego Rivera fresco and "The Big Horn Ram" featured in the mural by Rivera. I also donated another relief sculpture to City College in 1985, making it the owner now of four of my pieces.

For my work I use the tree feller's double bitted axe and adzes, razor sharp, for about 80 per cent of the carving. I use chisels and gouges only when it is too difficult to use the axe. I use chain saws for felling trees, cutting them into sections, and for removing large chunks of wood, but never for the actual carving. Sculpture can be best expressed with hand controlled tools.

Some commissions may require specific subject matter or design, or I may get some ideas from the

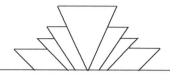

shape of the wood; again I might have a nightmare and dream up something. I trained myself to be versatile and to let my imagination take me in various directions. I have to keep my mind on the material with which I am working. Some wood or grain demands a certain treatment and some designs are more suitably executed in metal, stone, or other media.

At Treasure Island there were usually about half a dozen other artists working in the large area of the Fine Arts Building. We used to start at about ten in the morning and worked until ten at night. Mary Erchenbrack was doing a bust of Johnny Weissmuller. Weissmuller would come into my little cramped studio between the structural supports of the building and model for several of us. Helen Bruton was in charge of the Art in Action, and she and her sisters, Margaret and Esther, had executed "The Peacemakers" the previous year and continued to work there. So did others, including Cecilia Graham and Ruth Cravath. It was wonderful working there. About every other night after work several of us would take off for Chinatown. Diego Rivera was really good company. He could consume great volumes of red wine and always enjoyed himself. He was as good as a show, and helped everyone have a good time.

Diego had about ten helpers for his mural, but none helped him paint. Most of them would work at night mixing the fresco material. It took that long for it to be ready for paint. Then Diego would paint until it got too dry. I remember more than once he worked all day and all night because it stayed the right consistency. He would slowly move his huge physical bulk, 315 pounds, over the tiers of staging. If the result didn't satisfy his critical eye, he would have his helpers cut off the painted area, replaster it, and he would do it all over the next day, always demanding perfection in the work.

Because of international politics, some people, not understanding, objected to him and to his art. He would talk at great length about that. At one time in Mexico City Diego had kept Trotsky in his home for

> *Charles Laughton had trouble climbing to my 30-foot level to visit. My narrow passageway was not wide enough for his wider waistline.*

several years. Eventually they didn't see eye to eye about what socialism should be, and Trotsky moved out of Diego's home. After that they didn't associate much. Then in August, while we were working at the Fair, Trotsky was assassinated in Mexico. We were all afraid, that because Diego and Trotsky had been at one time such good friends, Diego's life would be in danger. It troubled him, too, and extra guards were assigned to our building.

In the central part of his huge mural Diego painted me working on "The Big Horn Ram." He put me into the mural three times; he wanted to show me as a forest engineer, as a logger, and as an artist. I remember his wife, Frieda, posing for her part of the mural. I told her I was flattered to keep her company in the mural. She said, "No, Señor! To me, it is one great privilege to be keeping company with you."

In some ways Diego and I were very much alike, and in some ways we were very different. We both had a natural passion to work on a large scale. We both found we could learn more from the primitive background of our own countries than we could from following modern trends in this country and abroad. He had had a good education and had studied extensively in all parts of the world. But it was in Mexico from the poor peasants that he learned about fresco mural painting. I was self taught only, but had the experience of being a frontiersman and the opportunity to observe the primitive art of the Northwest Indians. Like the Indians, my family made everything—our log houses, canoes, building materials, furniture, musical instruments.

Physically, Diego and I were very different. He weighed 315 pounds, while I weighed 122 pounds. His work required the ability to wield a paint brush weighing only a few ounces, while my work required the wielding of a tree feller's double bitted axe, attacking a 30-ton redwood tree trunk and manipulating the hand-operated elevator encircling it.

Diego had many wives and concubines, while for me one woman was the limit. My late wife and I

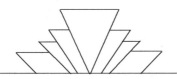

celebrated our golden wedding in 1972.

All of us artists at the Fair worked hard to attain our objectives, and we found it very encouraging to operate in such an open and friendly atmosphere. It was really evident that we all enjoyed participating in that exciting show.

I am often asked questions about my work and my age — how at 97 I enjoy good health and still work hard every day. I believe the spiritual side of life is important and that man should live closer to nature the way man is designed to live. The automobile has robbed us of our most natural form of exercise, walking. We are tempted by competitive markets to eat more than we really need and to buy foods that are not natural. Even though my father's family for years grew sugar cane in Barbados, I think sugar tempts us and we use

> *We both found that we could learn more from the primitive background of our own countries than we could from following modern trends.*

more of it than we need. I eat meat, plenty of fruits, especially apples, and plenty of vegetables. I have not required medical attention (except for injuries), nor have I taken a pill for more than 60 years. Except for six days of vacation I still work every day, using my double bitted axe.

Some of my work is displayed in the one-and-a-half-acre park surrounding my home and studio in Redmond, Washington. I always welcome people to come around and see the work I'm engaged in, other projects yet to come, and the growing collection here. *The Washington Centennial* has paid me a great tribute in stating that I am one of the top 100 people the state has produced in the first 100 years of statehood. I feel a great responsibility to the state to keep up a high standard of work, and not let it down.

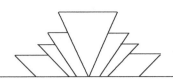

FRANCES KOCJAN SCARLETT

I was born in 1919 at home on York Street in San Francisco. I credit my interest in art to a man who roomed in our house. He had fought for the North in the Civil War and had seen Lincoln. Before he went into the service, he used to design carvings for furniture — scrolls, oak leaves, that sort of thing. I liked the fluid lines of the things he drew, and I would draw them, too, on the blackboard in our kitchen. I guess I was in the sixth grade when he passed away. I treasure my memory of that man. He used to say, "They will never build a Golden Gate Bridge," and now he is buried in the Presidio overlooking the Bridge.

When I was in junior high I started to do portraits on my own. Faces intrigued me. I would do portraits of the movie stars. As a senior in high school I designed the emblem for our senior sweaters. The bulldog was our mascot, and my drawing of it was voted the best; it was quite an honor.

After high school I took a correspondence course in art, and at the same time went to night school where

Frances Kocjan Scarlett, a sketch artist on the Gayway, still occasionally is commissioned to paint or sketch. She now lives in Belmont, California.

I studied portrait painting.

In 1939 I saw in the newspaper that a man named Claude Bell wanted to hire girls who were talented in portraiture to work at the Fair. I took some of my work over to Oakland where he was living. He thought my pictures were great, so I was hired. He was looking for people who could do a good likeness, and he wanted young girls. I was 20 at that time. His concession was going to be on the Gayway and he didn't want any fellows or older women.

He was a sand sculptor and he had had a stand in Atlantic City. Our spot at the Fair was outdoors, right next to a mind-reader near the entrance to the Gayway. The mind-reader would get a crowd together by asking his blindfolded wife questions like, "What am I holding in my hand?" Of course she would know the cues ahead of time. After a while the crowd would drift over to us.

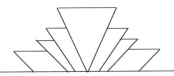

We were down in a somewhat sandy pit. The concessionaire had done murals covering the walls from one end of our property to the other. Then he built three-dimensional copies of paintings out of cement mixed with sand — famous paintings like "The Helping Hand" and "The Spirit of '76." He had a beautiful statue of King Neptune in the center; it was part of a fountain with fish and turtles spouting water. Behind this was a cave-like area where he and his wife had an office.

People would stand behind a railing and could see what we were doing because we were a bit lower. We did profiles that took just a few minutes each. Then we would write on the bottom, "Answer to a maiden's prayer," "Daddy's darling" — things like that. We did the outline in charcoal and worked with colored chalk to color in the hair, the cheeks a bit, and make a suggestion of a lapel or the top of a dress. We used newsprint. The main thing was to get a good likeness.

There was a four-foot by six-foot framed canvas area on the sandy ground near each stand where the customers would throw tips. They didn't have to pay for their pictures, but tips were encouraged. That's how we got paid every day. One third of the money was ours, one third went to the concessionaire, and one third to the Fair. I made about $40 a week. That was quite good for the time. In fact, on my next job I made only $18 a week.

There were four of us working at a time. Sometimes we'd be there until two in the morning. We would work for two hours at a time, and then get two hours off. In my time off I used to go to one of the shows or just sit and rest my legs, maybe have something to eat, and watch the people walk by. I liked to go to the Chinese Village where they had the most wonderful pineapple pie. I got acquainted with some of the people

> *People would stand behind a railing and could see what we were doing because we were a bit lower. We did profiles that took just a few minutes each.*

there. In fact, when the Fair closed, one of the barkers of the Chinese Village, Woody Louie, gave me his red satin jacket and black round cap. I didn't get to other areas of the Fair on the days I was working because we had to be back in two hours and couldn't be late.

I met a girl there who is still my best friend. She started the same time I did — Jean Grabe Shook. We've been best friends now for almost 50 years.

The day after the Fair closed, Jean and I went over for the last time. It was just like someone had died. There was no music; everything was quiet. There weren't many people, just those connected with the Fair finishing up what they had to do. I remember we each took some slips of pelargonium and had them in our gardens until they eventually died.

Years later in 1942 when I met my husband, he said he had been at the Fair and that I had drawn his picture. He had saved it, and even though we didn't sign our names, I knew I had done it. Everybody draws differently; it is just like handwriting.

After the Fair I worked at the Royal Flocking Company down at Second and Market where I painted little statues of animals. Later I worked as an artist and designer for the Paramount Flag Company. We made the flags from start to finish that were used in the Opera House at the beginning of the United Nations.

When I was raising my two daughters I didn't do any art work, but later I went back to it and worked for the nice Swiss people who ran the Hillsdale Gallery which later became The Bader Gallery. They sold many of my watercolor paintings there but lost their lease and had to close. Now I work at Mervyn's and I'm pretty tired when I get home, so I don't paint very much anymore.

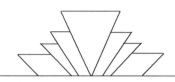

DOROTHY DEVINE

Dorothy Devine worked as a salesgirl at the White House, a San Francisco department store, until she left that to spend full time at home with her husband and sons.

The Fair was a wonderful place for dating. I was engaged when the Fair opened and married by the time it closed. Mr. Devine was an Elk, and the Elks had their Elk Day. They also were in charge of the Flag Day ceremonies. On these occasions they would pass out pamphlets and give little talks which ended with a sorrowful thing about their absent brothers. The absent ones were probably around the corner at some bar.

Hilo Hattie was a favorite of mine, possibly because I used to know her. She was a school teacher in the Islands, and during the Fair she sang with Harry Owens's Band at the Pacific House. I don't think you had to pay to see them. If you did, the prices were very reasonable. She sang funny little songs, naughty songs. But she was charming, a very gracious lady. She was large and a had a beautiful Hawaiian face, a gorgeous face. You might remember her from "Hawaii 5-0." She used to be on the early episodes.

Everything at the Fair was interesting, Billy Rose's Aquacade, the Chinese Village, the Carnation exhibit with the electric milking machines, the Marimba Band, the very ultra Lafayette House, the fireworks at night. So many things! It was a wonderful place.

Closing night of the Fair was perhaps the most moving time for all of us. Who would have thought it marked the end of an era and the beginning of hard times with WWII. I remember going with my husband up to Telegraph Hill to watch the lights go out on Treasure Island. Soon after, we would go to the same spot to see ships depart for the South Pacific. Ironically, after both San Francisco world fairs, we had to deal with world wars.

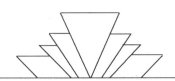

BARNEY GOULD

I began my rather checkered career as a newspaperman by editing the newspaper for Oakland's University High School. I went on to Stanford and edited the *Chaparral*, the campus humor magazine, and, after graduating, worked with the *Tribune* and the *Chronicle*. Later I made a connection with the *Hollywood Reporter*, a show business daily, and was their San Francisco correspondent during the Fair.

Back in 1939 I wrote in the *Hollywood Reporter* that the Fair was "beautiful but dumb." Artistically it was wonderful, but one dumb move of many was to place the Cavalcade of the Golden West, an elaborate and well acted outdoor spectacle, on the northernmost part of the Island, away from the Fair's high walls that provided protection from the wind. Despite the Cavalcade and the Folies Bergère, the '39 Fair was a disastrous flop financially. However, the exhibitors and others with huge investments badly wanted it to open for a second year.

I had been to New York to see Broadway shows

Barney Gould, a playwright, newspaperman, and press agent, brought the Aquacade to the Fair in 1940 by courting Billy Rose on behalf of the Fair's organizing committee.

and had met Billy Rose. He was a short man, but charged with energy. He was creative and dynamic with solid theatrical successes. One such was the Aquacade at the New York World's Fair, starring his wife, Eleanor Holm. I was able to convince him that his Aquacade would be a spectacular success in San Francisco in 1940. He agreed to open a West Coast show and, as it turned out, the show helped to save the Fair.

Billy Rose wrote this about me in the Aquacade program: "In The City That Knows How, I wanted to find a newspaperman who knows how to survey the local scene. And that's Barney Gould, San Francisco's theatrical reporter. Barney has been battling to get me to the Golden Gate International Exposition since 1937. So here we are, in the 1940 San Francisco Fair, with the Aquacade that played to 5 million customers in New York in 1939. And Barney is still in there pitch-

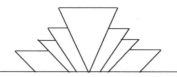

ing."

We played host to Billy and his staff in our family home on Twin Peaks — a former farmhouse overlooking the city down Market Street — and we showed the New Yorkers what a spectacular place they'd come to.

Rose's chief was a humorous Hoosier-type, Lincoln Dickey, and the house manager was big, jovial Irishman, Emmett Callahan. The designer was Clark Robinson, and Dinty Doyle, a colorful Irishman and bawdy storyteller, handled publicity. Apparently Billy thought he needed an old-timer to back me up in my role as publicist. Dinty spent a good deal of his time at Breen's with his many newspaper friends. Breen's was a wonderful saloon on Third near Mission — now, alas, gone.

Billy Rose had discovered a champion swimmer, 17-year-old Esther Williams, to be the "Eleanor Holm" of the San Francisco show. She starred along with Johnny Weissmuller, the singer Morton Downey, champion divers, and knockabout comedians. It was Dinty's and my job to get Esther's picture in all the

> *An exuberant Fair executive tried to sell him a lagoon site for his Aquacade. Billy put his finger in the wind and said, "No, gentlemen. I want an indoor Aquacade."*

papers, which wasn't difficult, as my voluminous scrapbook will show! She was a charming girl and quite beautiful. Esther married her childhood sweetheart, Leonard Lovner, a medical student, which gave me a news feature just after the Aquacade opened. As everyone now knows, Esther Williams followed her Aquacade triumph with starring roles in many MGM motion pictures.

One interesting note about the show-wise Billy Rose is the time when an exuberant Fair executive tried to sell him a lagoon site for his Aquacade. Billy put his finger in the wind and said, "No, gentlemen. I want an indoor Aquacade." He then selected an empty exhibit palace by the Fair's entrance for the huge amphitheater.

So the financial success of the second year of the Fair was largely due to the pulling power — right through the Fair's gates — of the Aquacade. I'm still proud, a half-century after my original brainstorm, that I convinced Billy Rose to illuminate Treasure Island.

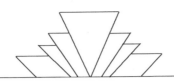

OLIVER APPLEGATE

World Fairs have been one of my special hobbies starting with the Lewis and Clark Exposition in Portland in 1905. I was nine years old then and very impressionable. I can remember all the details — just how the grounds were laid out and what was in each building. I've been Fair-conscious ever since.

I came to California from Oregon to see the '15 Exposition in the Marina in San Francisco. When I got to the Oregon Building I saw some of my drawings on the wall. The winter before my senior year in high school I had made some architectural renderings because at the time I wanted to be an architect. The school sent the drawings to the State Board of Education in Salem, and they thought they were good enough to send to the '15 Exposition in San Francisco. But I didn't know anything about that; I just walked in and there the drawings were.

I borrowed $10 from an older sister to get to that Exposition and I would go in from the time it opened

Oliver Applegate visited the Fair 100 times and recorded on film what he saw. He is retired now after having worked for many years for Standard Oil of California.

until it closed. I subsisted on sample handouts in the Food Palace. In my opinion, architecturally that Fair was far superior to any other fair that has ever been in the United States. It was far and away the most beautiful. Most of the exhibits were not too hot, but they had the Liberty Bell displayed right there on the street. The Fine Arts Palace of that Fair is still standing and testifies to the beauty of the exposition.

I was working in Sacramento but still looking for the right job. When I first applied at Standard Oil, they had only one job opening — for a male stenographer. I told them I was a male stenographer. I always say, "I was half-right; I was a male." I didn't get that job, but they called me a short time later and had a job for me which led to sales promotion work. When I went to work for them on January 29, 1917, they were still delivering gasoline with horse drawn equipment.

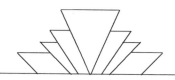

By about 1919 I was made head of the sales promotion department in Sacramento, and I came up with a successful idea for their exhibit at the State Fair. In 1930 I was promoted to the Home Office in San Francisco. Since then, through my term of life with Standard, I handled fairs and shows in addition to my other duties. So that just fit with my interest in fairs.

I went to the Chicago Fair in '33 and '34 because I knew I was going to be heavily involved with the San Diego World's Fair in '35. I wanted to see if I could pick up any ideas. I did pick up one I used at a state fair, but it was not world fair class. The exhibits in the buildings in Chicago were nicely done, but the architecture was very mediocre in my opinion.

San Diego had had a fair in '15 coincidental with the San Francisco one and the main concourse was very beautifully done. For their '35 Fair, they used those buildings again. The part of the Fair where my building, the Standard Oil Building, stood was the modern part. I call it "my" building because it was totally my responsibility — the design and construction as well as the exhibit inside. I am prejudiced, but I think it was the most striking building there, and I would be lying if I said I thought anything at the Golden Gate International Exposition in '39 and '40 could outdo it.

Ted Huggins, a very good friend of mine, was a natural born promoter. He had been hired by what is now Chevron — it was the Standard Oil Company of California — in the Public Relations Department. I think because the San Diego Fair was fresh in his mind when they built Treasure Island as an airport, he thought it would be a swell idea before it got into operation to have a world's fair there. He could be called "The Father of the Exposition."

I was in attendance at one of the preliminary meetings because I was in charge of all of Standard's participation in fairs and shows for the seven Western states. At the Treasure Island Fair, however, the oil companies all decided to go together for a big exhibit and bought $137,000 worth of space. They tried their

Well, there's nothing here but all this beauty.

best to hire me away from Standard to think up the ideas and run their exhibit. I declined; I didn't want to leave Standard for the three years that would have taken.

The major contribution I made in connection with the '39-'40 Fair was a movie I produced. I say I produced it because most of the shots are mine, but not all. I planned the movie to show the visual highlights — the plantings and the shows. I thought everything there was in good taste. I met a man from New York one day over there, and he was bragging about the World's Fair in New York. I said, "Don't you think we have a pretty good Fair here?" And he said, "Well, there's nothing here but all this beauty."

I was determined to record the beauty of the Fair as well as the excitement of the shows. At the performances I shot from the front row or from behind the back row, being careful not to let the noise of the camera bother anyone.

Remember Jo-Jo the Clown? He had been a hobo, and he decided to go back to hoboing when the Fair closed. It is my understanding that he left his wife and divorced himself from civilization. Life was too complicated for him. Before he left, he saw that I got his films of the Fair. He felt they were of considerable historical value. I think he had seen me over there many times taking movies, so he wanted me to have them. They are part of my film now. He also made movies of the burning of the California Building, but I didn't include them in my film because I didn't want anything negative. That fire is the only negative thing I connect with the Fair.

I wanted to be generous with my film, so I did let TV stations make copies of it. The woman who produced a film about Dudley Carter borrowed some shots from it. I lent her my original film, and she took it to Hollywood and used the shots she wanted. Lyle Bramson had a copy made for the museum at Treasure Island. Everyone is delighted now that these films were made. The original film is about a half century old and not available for copies now.

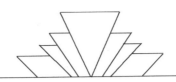

RALPH CAPPS

Ralph Capps, at age 14, was the youngest dancer at the Aquacade. He is now senior partner in the Walnut Creek law firm of Capps, Staples, Ward, Hastings and Dodson.

Jefferson High School in Daly City had a good group that played big band style and I started tap dancing with them before I graduated from grammar school. I had taken dancing lessons since I was nine years old. My parents were poor and it was tough, but I persisted. Darned if I know why.

I was 14 when I heard the Aquacade was going to be at the Fair and was looking for swimmers. I went over with my swimsuit thinking I'd try out, and I bumped into a couple of dancers I knew from McLean Dancing Studio. They suggested I try out as a dancer for the Aquacade instead. So I did.

The first tryouts were at the Civic Auditorium in San Francisco. There must have been 2000 male dancers auditioning there. At first they had us walk ten at a time up on the stage and said, "You step back. You step back." They eliminated the first two thirds, I think, just on looks and physique. Then they marched us up about five at a time to do time steps. There were four or five guys watching us and deciding

who to eliminate. Then we had five or six sessions in hotel rooms they had rented, until it got down to the 20 or 22 they wanted. Then it was back to the Civic Auditorium and Billy Rose was there. He had brought dancers up from Hollywood and said he would choose only four of us. He asked me to do the spins. I never was any good at ballet, and I fell, literally fell on the floor. He said, "Thank God I won't have to ask you to do that again. Step over here." And I thought I was out. But "over here" was the people he had selected. I guess he liked my smile after I fell.

"Jeffie," Lauretta Jefferson, was the one who really taught us the basics. She had worked with Billy Rose previously. She named me "Donald Duck" because of the way I kicked with my toes out and heels in. She liked to give nicknames to all the dancers. Our rehearsals were long and varied from day to day, about eight to twelve hours a day. It seemed to me we had

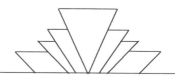

less than a month before the show opened.

I was by far the youngest. Just before the show opened they discovered I wasn't 18. They said, "They're not going to let the show open! Why didn't you tell us you were only 14?" So I went to the Child Labor Department, and I had to get a permit from them, and the high school principal had to approve. He rearranged my high school schedule so my classes were all in the morning. Two of us from Jefferson High made the show, myself and an older girl, Barbara Davis.

The show opened with the Fair. We usually did three shows a day and four on Saturdays and Sundays. I made $40 a week. My Dad, working in the technical department of the Fuller Paint Company, was supporting a family of seven on $45. He was happy for me. I gave some of my salary to the family and I put some aside for me.

There were 20 male dancers and twice as many female dancers. In addition there were showgirls, swimmers, divers, Fred Waring's choral group, stars, and specialty acts. One of my dancing partners was Miss Burlingame. She thought she was the greatest dancer in the world. There was some professional jealousy there. I remember in the final part of one scene I was to jump up and down, put my hands out, and the two girls I was dancing with were each to take one of my hands and do a backbend on the ramp which surrounded the huge pool. Well, this day Miss Burlingame dug her fingernails into my hand as she grabbed it. I let go and down she went. Her fall echoed throughout the 7,000 seat-theater. She got up and, as I was dancing off the stage, she pushed me into the water. Fortunately, I'm a good swimmer. I came up to the top and I heard people laughing so I swam with a nice stroke off underneath the stage while the audience applauded. The wardrobe lady had to get my wet clothes dry and ready for the next show.

We had what we called "The Been-in Club." On one of the walls backstage we wrote the names of the people who had gone into the pool by mistake. The most frequent ones were the couple on the tandem bicycle. They had a very tight turn to make and they went in probably six times. That wasn't really so bad considering the number of shows.

> *I never was good at ballet, and I fell, literally fell on the floor.*

I went in a couple of other times, myself. Once when I was looking for a friend in the audience, I slipped into the water. Another time I simply stepped back too far, not realizing how close I was to the edge of the narrow ramp. And then I went into the water the last night. The finale was timed so that just as the rest of us walked around the stage, Johnny Weissmuller would come out on one side and Esther Williams on the other. Johnny used to clown around a lot and he would often make us wait there marking time while he stood in the wings. A couple of times we would squirt him with a water gun when he did that. So on the final night when he finally got on stage, I followed him to squirt him. Instead he gave me a shove and in I went. Then he picked up singing star Morton Downey and threw him in the water. That was the ending of the whole Aquacade.

Johnny Weissmuller was very sociable. He was like a big kid. He had a yacht stationed at the Island and partied there with some of the cast. I never got invited as I was pretty young. My association with him was always backstage or in the water. I loved to swim. Between shows I swam a lot and he would come and work out and often gave me pointers on speed swimming. Esther Williams did the same on stylish swimming. She was very nice. This was her first professional show so she didn't display feelings of superiority.

We had a steady stream of celebrities coming backstage to see Weissmuller, and they all wanted to meet Esther Williams. I remember Jackie Cooper, Edgar Bergen, Anthony Quinn, and Shirley Temple coming around. I had an autograph book, but I eventually felt kind of silly using that because everybody knew celebrities around there. I got 30 or 40 autographs and then I quit.

There was a sadness at the end. I sawed off the "Been-in Club" wall (it turned out it was a big piece of plywood) and took it home with me. I tacked it on the wall downstairs in our home in Daly City. It might even still be there. My four older brothers and I all went into the service around '43 and my parents moved.

I learned a lot from the experience, but I was still

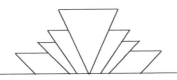

R ALPH C APPS

a regular teenager when it was all over. Jefferson High School was a small school and they had been kind of proud that they had two people in the Aquacade. I played basketball and football, organized the swimming team, helped out on the school aquacade, and tap danced with the band. When I became student body president, I was responsible for the half-hour assembly every day. We had speakers, movies, some humor sometimes, and rallies. Often I put on a show and I had free rein in doing this. I thought I had to tell a joke every day, and I soon ran out of material. I then took jokes out of my father's magazines. I remember one: "Those Jap zeroes are like a pair of step-ins. Takes only one yank to bring them down." I envisioned things on a clothes line. The principal called me in: "No more jokes."

I graduated from high school early, after three and half years, and a few days afterwards I joined the Navy. I was 17. I wanted to get over there and fight. Instead the Navy put me on a mine sweeper that was stationed on Treasure Island. At first we'd go out and sweep the channel everyday. Then we patrolled the Pacific Coast, getting into Monterey every 30 days.

> *This day Miss Burlingame dug her fingernails into my hand as she grabbed it. I let go and down she went.*

After the war I decided not to pursue dancing as a career. For one thing, I had torn a cartilage in high school playing football. It required an operation and the schools didn't cover that sort of thing at that time. Also after World War II there weren't many opportunities for tap dancers. Instead I went to college and majored in physical education, thinking I would be a coach.

I married my high school sweetheart, Lois Rich, and our first child was born while I was in college. I got into an automobile accident and didn't have any insurance. I learned the value of insurance and something about the law. I thought I'd gotten taken in that case. So I became an insurance adjuster and went to law school at night. Now I'm president and senior partner of the law firm, Capps, Staples, Ward, Hastings and Dodson in Walnut Creek.

I got out the old tap shoes early this year. I thought it'd be good exercise, that it would be kind of fun. I know I could teach myself again if I could knuckle down, but it took me awhile to figure out that it is not so much the old bones as it is the weight. I don't hop around like Twinkle Toes anymore.

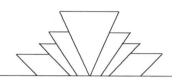

CLYDE DEVINE

It was in the Reno, Nevada, YMCA that I learned to swim. I was eight years old at the time and tall for my age, so they let me in the class. The second day I dived off the board. Just took off. I love the water.

Later, my dad, who worked for Swift and Company, was transferred to South San Francisco, where we had lived originally. I could swim only in the summers then, at the San Mateo County Boy Scout Camp at Pescadero. I was in Troop #161, and since I was the tallest guy around at the scout camp, they made me life guard. The year after I was graduated from Burlingame High a pool was put in, but I missed out on that.

I had a football scholarship to Oregon State and there I was on the swimming and football teams. After I graduated, I got a job teaching at San Rafael Military Academy. I didn't have my complete teaching credential yet, but when I earned it, I went to Sequoia High School in Redwood City where I taught and coached for 40 years. Twenty of those years I also worked part time as a diving coach at Stanford University.

I heard about the Aquacade through the *Chronicle*. Two seniors from Sequoia High, Harry Killpack and Ted Cole, were also interested, so the three of us hopped in a car and off we went to look around. When we got to the Civic Auditorium in San Francisco where the auditions were to be held, the swimmers were all told to show up the next morning at six at the Fairmont Hotel and about 500 of us did. I had to be back in Redwood City at 9:30 for school so I was a little afraid I'd be late. But I wanted to be in that Aquacade!

There was a pool in the Tonga Room there, and we were told to swim laps, two by two. It was well organized. Some people were eliminated right away, and every morning the rest of us would arrive and continue the tryouts. It was just like the 49er players getting cut. "See ya later." Big tears, you know.

I think they picked me because I was the tallest

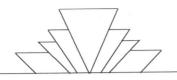

person there and because of my stroke. I am what you call a sea horse, a heavy swimmer. Killpack and Cole also made the cut.

Once we were picked and signed the contract, we practiced at Crystal Plunge in North Beach. The pool at Treasure Island wasn't ready until just before the Fair opened in 1940. It was something to see how they threw that pool together. It was wooden, of tongue-in-groove construction.

We were all nervous opening day, but we were psyched up. We did well and congratulated ourselves. "Nice going, gang." The audience raved about the show from the start, especially the rainbow dive. Fifty-six of us, one at a time, would dive off the stage. We would dive deeply, ten feet into the dark water. The visibility wasn't great in this wooden tank. There was a white block for each of us to grab hold of, a two by four, and we would then put our feet on it and go shooting up the ten feet to the surface. The audience would see fluorescent caps coming up, bing! bing! bing! From that we went into what they call four-four; four strokes and then on to the backstroke for four.

We always had a full house — the natatorium held 16,000 people. A few times there were drunks in the audience who came to close to the pool and fell in. There were no barricades, just a rail. As we swam, we would check the audience to see if we knew anyone there. If my wife was coming, I'd look for her and give her a little dipsy-doodle-hi.

We did three routines, 15 minutes each, three or four times a day. Some of the swimmers didn't take care of themselves and had wet ear canals all day long. Health was a problem; to keep us from getting erysipelas, a big rule was posted. We had to use alcohol and glycerin to lubricate and medicate our ears.

I was fairly concerned about having two jobs. I signed the contract with the Aquacade while I was under contract at Sequoia High. My wife had just had a baby and I needed a good summer job; I needed the income. The pay was a lot of money — $60 a week. I managed to do both jobs by paying another teacher to take my afternoon classes at school. I had to leave Redwood City at 11 in the morning to catch the #40 street car that took me into San Francisco and to the ferry. Then the ferry got me to the Island on time for the 2:30 matinee.

After the show opened the *Chronicle* ran a pic-ture of Killpack, Cole and me coming out of the water. It was a very clear picture, very good. "Nice going, Clyde," said my P.E. boss, but the principal wasn't pleased. He called me in. "Hey, what's this? You can't get out of school for this." He couldn't really give me permission even if he wanted to because the faculty would not have understood. They would get a little jealous of anyone who did something different. But my arrangement with the other teacher worked out, and in about a month the school summer vacation started.

I was very impressed with the divers in the show. They were Olympic champions and nice guys. Sometimes, when one of them was sick, I would substitute. I would do something easy, and they were good about showing me how to do the things they were doing. In the Olympics at that time the biggest dive was a front somersault with one twist. Here these guys, Sammy Howard, Larry Griswold, Marshall Wayne and Alfie Phillips were doing split two-and-a-halfs, three-and-a-halfs — unheard of then.

I substituted for Johnny Weissmuller twice. He was terrific, like an aquaplane. He kicked up a big splash for effect especially when he swam behind Esther Williams in a number they did together. She was supported on his hips, and they swam like a couple of frogs.

She was a beautiful girl, but she was knock-kneed. They taught her how to stand so her legs looked great. The movie people were often around to check her out, and after the Fair closed she went right down to Hollywood.

I went down there during the next three summers myself because I was getting my master's degree at the University of Southern California. Esther helped me get a part in a movie where I was one of a group of guys who took off from swings into a pool. That particular shot is in "That's Entertainment." I also was a surfer in "Ebbtide" and had bit parts in a couple of other movies. We got paid $11 a day, $13 if we said anything. I never made $13.

During all those years at Sequoia High I had different things going — the Aquacade, swimming schools, coaching, refereeing 49er games, and putting on swim shows at places like the Menlo Circus Club. Sometimes I'd have too much going on, but I've enjoyed it all. I live in Reno now and I'm still working around water, teaching children to swim and dive.

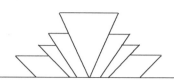

SAL DeGUARDA

My family came out to Oakland from New Jersey when I was three. I was still in high school when the Fair opened in 1939, but my friends and I didn't have the money to get there. If you went over from Oakland, you paid for the ferry boat and the Fair admission at the same time — when you got on the Island. My friends and I would take the ferry and when the boat docked, we'd go hand-over-hand under the pier and climb up on the other side of the entrance and walk on for free. Once one of my friend's feet hit the water, so he was slushing around the whole time we were there. Later, when I was part of the Aquacade, I used to comment on how nice it was to go on the Island without having to sneak on.

When I was about to graduate from high school, Buck Shaw came to my house and offered me a football scholarship to the University of Santa Clara. We were on the half-term system in Oakland and I got out of school in January, but I was to start college in September.

Sal DeGuarda, a swimmer at the Aquacade in 1940, went on to Hollywood where he appeared in several pictures. He has since been in the construction business.

Things were kind of slow, the Depression, you know, so a friend and I rode the freight trains looking for work until September. I ended up in New Jersey where I had relatives, and I got a job with a roofing company. Then a friend of my cousin talked me into playing football for the Hackensack Steamrollers, a farm team for the New York Giants. At the roofing company I was making $20 a week and here I was getting $50 for each game. I thought I was a millionaire. So I said, "To hell with college. I'm going to be a football player." In the fourth game I wrecked my knee, and that put me out of football and out of any chance for the college scholarship.

When I got back home I read in the newspapers that they were going to have the Aquacade at Treasure Island, so I went to try out. The first thing they did was pick guys out for physique, and then we went up to the Fairmont Hotel to swim the length of the pool. When

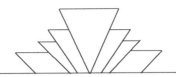

I dove in and started to swim, the fellow who was picking the swimmers said, "Out." So I swam to the side. Then he said, "In." I had been tense and probably didn't look good when I first got in the pool, and when I relaxed and swam to the side, he changed his mind about me.

We went through more eliminations. To a 4-count we would swim together — two, three, four at a time. So we were doing this synchronized swimming for free while the eliminations went on. When it came time for the dress rehearsals, for being hired and being on salary, we already knew the routines. That was pretty shrewd of Billy Rose. He was sharp. I met him only one day, but he knew exactly what he wanted. He was a showman. Esther Williams came there as just a little kid who swam, and he made her a star.

Esther Williams was naive, in a way. She wasn't a show-off. I was going with her the first part of the show, taking her out. Then later on she fell in love with a doctor and they got married for a short period of time.

The whole time of the Aquacade I never saw one fight or argument between anyone. It was like a close-knit family. There were the little romances and the love affairs; I'm talking about 250 people.

The performances themselves got to be routine, so there was always somebody doing something extra. We had a "Blue Danube" number where we wore fluorescent gloves and caps. As we swam out the lights would go out and stagehands would turn on the black lights which would show just the fluorescent gloves and caps. Well, the girls one day decided they were going to go topless. As they swam this number, they were going to pull their tops down. I heard about it and sent word up to the guy on the lights and as soon as we got going he turned the lights back up. The girls scrambled down in the water to get those tops back on.

Once in awhile I filled in on the comedy diving, but usually I just swam. I could never have taken points in any kind of competition, but I had what you call a showman's stroke. One day my friend Clyde and I were practicing diving, and I hit the side of the pool. Clyde had to pull me out. A few years later, during the

> *I had a tux and tails on, and I thought I looked pretty sharp, and Mae West asked, "Where did you get those rags?"*

recruiting for the war, I found out that my vertebrae were all twisted from that accident. The doctor at the draft board said that probably the only thing that saved me was that I went on with the show. If I had lain down, the muscles and nerves in my back might have set, and then I would have been paralyzed from the waist down.

Although Esther became the star of the show, the big drawing cards at the start were Gertrude Ederle, Morton Downey and Johnny Weissmuller.

Gertrude Ederle, the first woman to swim the English Channel, broke the men's record when she swam it. She was a nice person, very much to herself because she was hard of hearing. I think she might have lost her hearing as a result of the channel swim. She could read lips, and she would use sign language with her companion. She was then in her early 30s, a little older than most of us.

1940 was a patriotic time. For the finale the girls would bring down a huge flag and Morton Downey would sing, "Yankee Doodle." I'd get goose pimples every time. Boy, it would just get you! On one side was Vincent Travers's Band with about 40 members and the other side was Fred Waring's Glee Club with about 20 singers. Even though we did the same thing every day I'd get a new thrill with that music and singing.

The last day we all were almost in tears. It was like the end of a beautiful romance that you walked away from.

After that I swam for the USO shows, worked in the shipyards, and coached at a boys' camp. The Hollywood producer, George Stevens, had his son in the boys' camp, and it was through him that I got into pictures.

I started as a stand-in double for Jon Hall. When I was working on "Ali Baba and the Forty Thieves," I was going with a girl who had a dance interview for a Mae West picture. I went to pick up my friend after the interview, and a fellow on the stage said, "Young man, up here." I said I wasn't there for the dance interview, but he said, "No, I want you here for a part in the picture." I went up, but I couldn't believe this was happening to me! A couple of days later I signed a

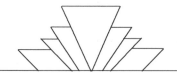

contract for $600 a week. I was so nervous, it took two hands to sign the thing. It was for a Mae West picture.

After that picture I had an interview with Otto Preminger. I got in line with the rest of the guys, and when I got to Otto Preminger, he said, "Name?" I said, "Sal DeGuarda." He said, "Nationality?" I said, "Italian." He said, "Sorry." So I got in the same line again, and when he came up to me the second time and said, "Name?" I said, "John Dexter." "Nationality?" "English, old boy." And I got the part. That was the way I became John Dexter.

I was with Mae West in "The Heat's On" — a small part. If you blinked your eyes you would miss me. I remember the first day I came on the set. I had a tux and tails on, and I thought I looked pretty sharp, and Mae West asked, "Where did you get those rags?" She called the assistant director over and said, "Get the boy dressed. I don't want wardrobe clothes; I want them custom made." She was 52 years old then and looked as sharp as any 30 year old would ever look. I remember sending her 52 roses for her birthday. I think I was 23.

She was very nice, a very sharp woman. I lived with her for quite a while. She told me her sex drive

> *A few years later, during recruiting for the war, I found out that my vertebrae were all twisted from that accident.*

came because she had a double thyroid. She wrote all her own plays and changed the lines of the movies she was in. She wrote lines according to what she wanted and she got what she wanted. Business-wise she was the tops. She owned those Greyline buses that took people to see movie stars' houses, and she owned most of the ranches around Van Nuys. The last time I saw her she was 77. She pulled her hair back to show me she hadn't had a face lift.

Johnny Weissmuller used to say that he wanted me to be the one to replace him as Tarzan. That's the part I always wanted. Then, when he retired from that part, the studio signed Lex Barker for the role. I was married then, and my wife had been after me to leave the movies, and that seemed the time to do so. So I quit.

Then I went into the construction business with my brother, and although I've always kept up my swimming, I've been in the construction business ever since. From 1981-1985 I was building concrete houses here and in the Philippines. Working in the Philippines was another interesting experience. I lost everything when Marcos fled the country, but I take what happens just as another step in life, and enjoy whatever it is.

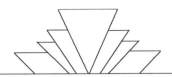

LEON DAVID ADAMS

Leon David Adams, the noted writer on wine who started the Wine Institute, organized California wineries to build and operate the Wine Temple at the Fair.

I was a San Francisco journalist, often a waterfront reporter, until 1937. Since the early '20s I have been interested in the most important industry in California — wine. During twenty of the last fifty-odd years I have organized and operated The Grapegrowers League of California and The Wine Institute.

As a newspaper man I covered the professional prohibitionists. Profit motivates people, and they were making prohibition profitable. The people who put up the money were motivated by the idea of doing good. There is a psychological element here. By stopping another individual's pleasure, one feels the thrill of doing some good. An example of this goes back to rearing infants. It gives parents a pleasant feeling to stop a child from doing what is wrong.

Early in this country members of the clergy would go from home to home where the families served something to drink. The future Dries discovered the pleasure of saving the clergy from excessive drinking. That was the origin of the prohibition movement. It was a happy day for me when on December 5, 1933, prohibition was repealed.

Besides originating organized wine education in America, I have always been interested in civic projects. So, when the idea was brought up in the '30s that San Francisco needed an airport, that got my attention. It was suggested that the mud flats by Yerba Buena Island become the San Francisco Airport. Since I had once conducted a harbor bond campaign, I talked to influential people about getting the mud flats ceded to the city so they could be filled. There had been some opposition from people in San Mateo County who knew that the mud flats were not large enough for an airport, but it was exciting when the mud flats were filled to accommodate airplanes.

When the mud flats were being filled, that's when my friend Ted Huggins of Standard Oil said we ought to have a World's Fair. Ted was interested in everything that would be good for San Francisco. He was unselfish, and he had wonderful ideas. He has had a remarkable life. He is now 97. I am only 82. I was one of the people who greatly admired the 1915 Exposition and my boyhood memory of that added glamour

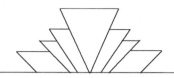

and attraction to the idea of having another Fair on the one time mud flats that had become the island.

I remember a luncheon given in July, 1938, in honor of President Roosevelt when he came to see the Fair site and the construction that was in progress. It was my privilege to choose the wines for that luncheon, and I carried a bottle of Inglenook Riesling to be served to him. The Secret Service would not let me pour it, but President Roosevelt drank and complimented the wine. Of course, he complimented many kinds of things.

I was enthusiastic about making wine an important part of the Fair. I was disappointed that we couldn't raise enough money to have a separate wine pavilion, like the one that had been part of the 1915 Fair.

> *The Secret Service would not let me pour it, but President Roosevelt drank and complimented the wine.*

The idea evolved to have a Wine Temple in the Agriculture Building. We called it "Temple" to give it a more spectacular name and to get additional attention. It was two stories high, impressive, and imposing. Upstairs we had wine tasting; downstairs we had wine exhibits behind glass. Each participating winery paid for its part of the cost and also supplied wine for tasting upstairs. Sometimes it was so crowded you couldn't get in, but we never had a single incident of intemperance or disorder.

Frank Whitely and Jessica McLaughlin Greengard were the people to whom credit for the success of the Wine Temple should be given. They were members of my Wine Institute staff, and my good fortune was in having found and helped capable people.

Graceful arches surrounded the serene Court of Flowers, designed by Lewis Hobart. Julius Girod, the head landscape engineer for the Fair, planned every detail of the complex horticultural layout. The first thing many people recall about the Fair is the splash of color from tens of thousands of flowers. Vivian Girod, Julius' widow, loved this spot best of all.

The towering 80-foot figure of Pacifica dominated the north end of the vast central promenade. Some people thought the statue looked too primitive in style, but others praised its stark power. Whether sculptor Ralph Stackpole intended it to look Mayan, Asian, or both is anybody's guess.

Above: Pacifica's backdrop of metal stars and tubes was a huge wind chime, floodlit at night with constantly changing colors. Sculptures surrounded the Fountain of the Western Waters at Pacifica's feet. A few pieces of sculpture survive; plans are in the works to restore the fountain and place it in front of Treasure Island's Administration Building.
Right: The vast perspective of the Court of the Seven Seas leads the eye to Pacifica at the far north end.

Top: "Young Man Improvising Music" by Adaline Kent reposes on the Fountain of the Western Waters.
Bottom: The wall behind the fountain honors the European explorers who sailed the seven seas.
Opposite: Esther, Helen, and Margaret Bruton, three sisters from Alameda, executed the splendid bas relief mural entitled "The Peacemakers," 57 feet high and 157 feet long, depicting a colossal 40-foot Buddha surrounded by Eastern and Western peoples and their architectural and cultural monuments such as the Great Wall of China and the Bay Bridge. The rolling chairboys liked to wait for fares in the courtyard.

Above: P. O. Tognelli's "Christopher Columbus" stands on a ship's prow over a doorway in the Court of the Seven Seas. In the foreground is Haig Patigian's "Creation."
Left: Olof C. Malmquist's Rainbow Fountain stands at the center the Court of Flowers.
Opposite: "Ocean Breeze" by Jacques Schnier, part of the Temple of the East, looks down on the Temple Compound where bands played every day. These pictures show the astonishing variety of sculpture at the Fair.

The Fountain of Life, fashioned by O.C. Malmquist, was at the center of the Court of Flowers. It rose 50 feet high with a 12-foot female nude holding a rainbow captured from the western sky. Mermaids, seals, and other sea creatures are grouped around the base. At night the floodlights shining through the water would create rainbows; most people called it the Rainbow Fountain. Far right: In the Treasure Garden at the south end of the Island, a great plume fountain rose from a reflecting pool. (Courtesy Treasure Island Museum)

Opposite: The daylight view of the Court of Flowers shows the graceful arches and curved forms of the fountains. Top: In a quiet corner of the Court of Flowers, the photographer's mother, Nina Jacob, rests for a moment. Bottom: The highly stylized lettering on the Sermons from Science Building was pure Art Deco. It contrasts with the Spanish Colonial architecture of the Colombian Building, where fresh coffee was served.

Opposite: The Japanese Pavilion was one of the most extensive of the foreign nations' exhibits. It included an elaborate garden (top), a feudal castle and Samurai house. The emperor's own gardener came over to install the garden, along with all workmen and materials for the exhbit. It was the focal point for many social functions hosted by the genial Consul-General and his wife.
Above: The Philippine Pavilion displayed native clothing, fruits and vegetables, and bamboo furniture. Zombies were the featured drinks at the Philippine bar.
Right center: The Hurtado Brothers Marimba Band was one of the most popular musical attractions at the Fair.
Lower right: Norway built typical log houses with grass growing from the sod roofs. Norwegian delicacies were served to visitors in front of a huge open fireplace. In 1940 Norwegians of the Bay Area took over the exhibit, since Norway had fallen to Hitler.

Above: The New Zealand Pavilion, a Maori meeting house with exotic carved decorations, displayed war canoes, flax skirts, and native handicrafts.
Left: The Chinese Village was funded by Chinese-Americans, whose homeland was fighting a war with Japan. A wall enclosed several buildings, including a very popular restaurant, a theater for acrobats and Chinese opera, an exhibit of priceless jade, and a special building for Princess Der Ling, the Empress Dowager's lady in waiting. (Courtesy Richard Reinhardt)
Opposite top: Pan American's China Clippers docked on the south side of the Island, just below the cantilever section of the Bay Bridge.
Opposite bottom: An S-curve of flowers leads the eye to the tower of the California Counties Building and the Bay Bridge beyond.

Overleaf: The statue of the Evening Star glows in the Court of the Moon.

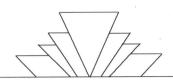

VIRGINIA O'LEARY BAKER

I was born and raised in San Francisco between 23rd and 24th Avenue in the Richmond, and was about 18 when I first started working at the Fair. My father had been a San Francisco police officer, and both he and my mother died young. I was living with my aunt when the Chief of Police called and asked my aunt if I would want to work at the Fair. He told her, "This is supposed to be nice, and I could get her in the Ghirardelli exhibit." The Chief had been a friend of my father; people really looked after each other then.

We were just coming out of the Great Depression, and it was hard to get work. People who lost their jobs went to the firemen and policemen they knew, asking them to take over their mortgages, because they were the only ones working. During the Depression when my father was alive, he used to pick up children off the streets and buy them shoes.

A lot of people came to San Francisco to work at the Fair from out of state; so many competed for jobs. To be hired I had to go to the waitresses' union and be interviewed. You had to be a certain weight and a certain height and look presentable. We even had to show how we walked. They wanted everybody to look uniform.

The opening day of the Fair was hectic; it was terrible. I had never seen anything like it in my life. The ferry boats were mobbed. People never stopped coming into our exhibit and we worked serving chocolate all day long.

The Ghirardelli exhibit was more of a place to advertise the product than to serve food. We wore spotless brown uniforms with checked cuffs and nice little aprons. When people came in, they were served a cup of chocolate, a cookie, and a candy bar — nothing else. My customers paid me, and I made the change. I went back and forth collecting money and serving chocolate. They had it running slick; nobody could get away with anything.

The exhibit was beautiful — like a tea room. They

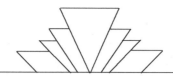

had murals of chocolate and the cocoa bean. Off to the side was a huge round machine, as big as a room, that stirred the chocolate. I was crazy never to have taken a picture of that chocolate as it went around. To tell you the truth, I was pretty nervous and hardly ever went over to look at that machine; that was for the tourists. I remember Loretta Young having chocolate at Ghirardelli's.

Our boss was a miserable woman. She was quite elderly and would never smile or say anything nice. She was just like an old schoolmarm. No matter how hard a person worked, she wanted more. It was like a strict convent. No job in those days was easy. But you needed the money, so you never complained.

After serving the chocolate all day, we didn't care to eat any. We were glad to get out of there and to go home and eat good food. I do still like chocolate and think Ghirardelli's is the best, but I don't think it is as good as it used to be.

The Fair was beautiful, gorgeous. Seeing it was a great experience; it was just like when a person goes to Disneyland for the first time. I remember the TV exhibit and thinking it was impossible that someday TV might be in my home.

Of course, I did not see too much of the Fair. After serving people all day, I was tired and didn't care to

> *People who lost their jobs went to the firemen and policemen they knew, asking them to take over their mortgages, because they were the only ones working.*

look around. A lot of the other girls would go out on dates after work, but I don't think they would have considered dating anybody from Ghirardelli's. My cautious Irish family told me to come home and not talk to a soul. I did meet one girl who worked as a hat check girl on another part of the Island; she became a life-long friend.

What I liked about the job was making some money. I put most of it in the bank and bought some clothes. I worked until October of that year. A lot of girls left after a couple of months. They knew the Fair was going to close. They had made their money and moved on.

Working at the Fair was my first job. From there I went to work for an automobile dealer. I married my husband, Joe, who was also raised in the City. He was a doorman at the Mark Hopkins Hotel which was a good job. We lived out on 20th Avenue and had two sons. When the war broke out I went to work for the telephone company.

When I look back I realize that I was lucky to have had the chance to work at the Fair. At the time I did not appreciate it. I was just trying to get some work and to get ahead. The tourists came and took advantage of the Fair, but I did not realize what was there until later in life. To think that I was able to be a small part of it is amazing to me now.

JOE BIZAL

I was born in 1914 in Kansas and lived there and in Oklahoma until 1937 when I came to San Francisco. At that time I was a four-year plumber's apprentice, but I had to do odd jobs because of the economy. When I applied for the job of selling Coca Cola at the Fair, I was just one of many. I think I got one of the jobs because I had had some experience selling soft drinks. My family had lived adjacent to a swimming pool where they owned a soft drink and candy stand. Sometimes I helped out at that stand.

In 1939 I lived in a boarding house at 962 Eddy Street; it was exciting living in San Francisco then. I made friends with the people who worked at the Fair and we often stayed on the Island after work. The climate was best there around midnight. I liked being on the fairgrounds; there was so much to see. People of all colors and races had festive attitudes.

Coca Cola had the soft drink concession at the Fair. The first year I worked at stand #25 at the corner of the Ford Building.

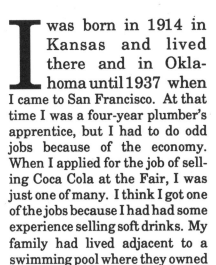

Joe Bizal sold Coca Cola at the Fair and supervised ten vendors. He later went on to work as a plumber and is now retired and living in Oroville.

I remember the day the Fair opened. It was cool, overcast with a high fog, and we were apprehensive. Was anyone going to come? Around noon people started to arrive. Most seemed to have set their sights for the Gayway. Do you know a Bay Area woman won $500 in a contest for naming that area? I remember entering a name, but I don't recall what it was, obviously not a winner.

Coca Cola came only in six-ounce bottles then. We kept them in Coca Cola coolers and the reserve supplies on ice in regular home wash tubs. Sometimes we would be swamped and other times to get business we would call out, "Get your Coca Cola here. Five cents!" It wasn't called "Coke" until years later.

Coca Cola is not an exotic drink, but it is a refreshing one. Sometimes people would mix rum with it. You'd see them do that. They might have their sandwiches and a bottle of rum with them, but that

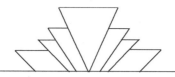

wasn't too common.

I never got sick of drinking Coca Cola. We were allowed two free bottles. I drank from eight to ten bottles a day, so I had to pay for most of them. Each man had to report the number of bottles he received and the amount of money he collected. You'd expect to break two bottles a day at least. Many times we had severe cuts on our hands from broken bottles in the coolers.

Across from my stand was a Guess-Your-Weight fellow. When his customer was a man, he would feel his arms, shoulders, and legs. Then he would go into a spiel that could be heard some distance; he guessed, then retracted what he guessed, felt again and finally gave his answer. When guessing the weight of a woman he would go through the same antics, but not touch her. After he had attracted a little crowd he would prove his ability by having the customer get on his sit-on scale. If he didn't guess the weight correctly within two pounds, he gave the customer a prize. When business was slow, he'd motion me over and I'd shill for him. He'd always guess my weight wrong, and I'd get a box of candy. Later I'd give the candy back. He was good at what he did, a real carnival performer.

The White Carnation Company had a flower stand where a beautiful young lady pinned a carnation on your lapel for ten cents. At the beginning of the day I would always stop there and receive a white carnation, compliments of the flower girl.

The Remington-Rand Company handed out electric razors to use. Quite a number of men were eager to try out this new idea in shaving. It was my first experience with an electric razor, and after I finished with it, the razor was put through a sterilization process to be available for the next gentleman to use.

The people at the Fair were very congenial — customers, too. When we heard different accents, we would ask the people where they were from. Some would be from Texas or back East. Some even were from my home town and were really surprised to see me there.

Coca-Cola had a bottling plant in the middle of H Building. I believe the northern end of that building

It was overcast with a high fog, and we were apprehensive. Was anyone going to come?

was a dance pavilion and the southern part was where Art Linkletter had his program. He interviewed people who came to the Fair, like a talk show today. The Coca Cola section was quite an attraction. The public could watch the bottles go to the sterilizer, then they would go along a conveyer to the filler, then to the capper, and last they went into the cases. The human hand didn't touch anything until the bottles were placed into wooden cases, 24 bottles to a case.

Between the two years of the Fair I worked part time repairing ships on the waterfront. That helped towards my apprenticeship.

I met my wife, Marie, in 1940. She was employed by E. I. DuPont Company in South San Francisco and she worked at DuPont's display, introducing nylon hosiery at the Fair. Many women received their first pair of nylons there, compliments of the DuPont Company.

When the Fair opened again in 1940 I was made a supervisor in charge of ten stands in the Gayway area. My job then was to make sure everyone was on the job to deliver needed supplies, collect reports from each stand, and to deliver the day's receipts to the cashier.

Coca Cola had an ice house on the Island, and we supervisors had to move ice around to the stands maybe four or five times a day, pushing it around in carts. Sometimes the Coca Cola moved so fast it wasn't completely chilled when it was sold.

The last day of the Fair was a warm one and bottling plants in the Bay Area were called to supply extra Coca Cola. We sold 9,000 cases that day — that's 24 bottles to a case. There was no bottle charge, and we always had to go around to pick up the bottles. People would leave them anywhere. When the Fair was over, I stayed and helped clean up. I remember when they drained the Lake of Nations, it was a foot deep with Coca Cola bottles.

Another thing that will remain with me forever is looking at the National Cash Register that last day of the Fair. It showed that over 200,000 people came to the Island that day.

GEORGE HUBBARD

I grew up working in a drugstore in Oklahoma, and when I came to California in '26 there were no job openings for pharmacists. I remembered what my pappy said: "Anytime you want to do an honest day's work for an honest day's pay, there's someplace in this world somebody wants you." It was true. I found work in the food service business for Heinz.

I was their salesman for hotels and clubs in San Francisco. In 1940 the Heinz management people called me and asked if I could also take over their interests at the Fair. The guy that they had there the first year was too busy enjoying himself at the Fair. Heinz had a big exhibit there and yet they weren't getting any business. So I said, "Sure, I can do it," and I did. I'd work the hotels and clubs in San Francisco in the mornings and then go over and work the Fair in the afternoons and evenings.

Every day I'd drive over and then walk all around to the restaurants with my leather bag and samples. By the time I had the ketchup, chili sauce and a couple

George Hubbard worked at the Fair for Heinz where he kept restaurants stocked with Heinz products. Retired, he now lives in San Francisco.

of kinds of soup, a hot thermos bottle to serve the soup, and a cold thermos for the tomato juice, well, it would weigh about 40 pounds. It was just a day's work.

The restaurants there got big money, hotel prices, San Francisco prices, for the food. I remember the fellow who had Bob's Steak House in San Francisco had a place over at Treasure Island. He also ran the booth that sold scones. They were very popular — scones and preserves, strawberry and blackberry. They were quite a big thing, something different.

As I was going from one restaurant to another, I'd stop a bit and listen to the music. The Hurtado Brothers' Marimba Band was world famous, and everyone who went by and heard them playing stopped for a while.

As you'd walk along, Candid Camera Men would take your picture with a German camera, Rolleiflex, I

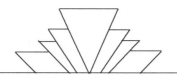

think, and give you a little paper that you could mail in for your picture. Not many people had their own cameras, so it was a nice thing.

I did get to see the Aquacade. It was a fabulous show. When Billy Rose brought in Esther Williams, that was the icing on the cake.

I was working all the time, and anything I saw was just in and out. Hills Bros. had a place where they showed how coffee is made, and you could actually smell the coffee as you looked at the pictures. Unbelievable. Someone said they piped in that fragrance of percolating coffee.

The barker outside Sally Rand's Nude Ranch had quite a gimmick. Inside there were girls with very little on and lots of little burros. The barker would yell, "Come and see Sally Rand's ass."

Around the Fair were chairs with wheels that older people could use and be pushed around the fairgrounds. Those chairs were one of the assets that made the Fair a success, 'cause when your feets hurt, you hurts all over.

Whenever anyone hears I worked for Heinz at the Fair, they ask me about the pickle pins. In days gone by when you wanted pickles, you went to the butcher shop where they sold them from a barrel. The clerk would dip in and get the pickles for the customers, a nickel for a pickle. The customer might also get a little

> *The barker outside Sally Rand's Nude Ranch had quite a gimmick. Inside there were girls with very little on and lots of little burros. The barker would yell, "Come and see Sally Rand's ass."*

baby pickle pin made of plaster of Paris. Now the pins are plastic.

The Heinz salesmen would carry these little pins around with them and when the owner of the store would ask for one, the salesman would usually say, "I happen to have one more. It's my last pickle. You can have it." Well, Heinz passed pickle pins out at the Fair. Frank Armour was in charge of that, and everyone who went to that exhibit got one of these baby pickle pins. The pins were popular with everyone; if youngsters had one to wear to school, why they felt just a bit exclusive. They felt like they were "in." Now, all these years later when I go to the reunions of the Fair employees, someone will come up to me and ask me if I happen to have a pickle pin with me. They want it for their granddaughter, a friend, or just for themselves. When they come up to me, I say, "You are in luck. I have one more pin. It's my last one, but you can have it."

When I was at the Fair I didn't give pins to the public, but I would hand them to the chef or the buyer at the restaurants I served. I liked my job. I tried to do a good job. I saw what had happened to the guy before me who didn't do his job. Good-bye baby. Not too many people today would work for a company in the mornings and then in the afternoons and evenings, too. It's not that the people are different. It's the world we live in. That's what makes the difference.

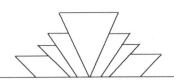

REGINA BRYMER

I was born and raised in San Francisco. I was about 21 when I quit my job in a creamery on Irving Street and went to work at the Fair selling caramel corn. I don't remember how I got that job in the Food Building, but I've never had trouble getting jobs, even now.

I was over there in the mornings as soon as the Fair opened to get the machine activated. I like sweets, but I get tired of them quickly. I don't remember eating much caramel corn. Somehow it would spout out of the machine during the day and it would get on the floor. One piece would stick to another, and pretty soon I had great big caramel corn feet. I brought other shoes to wear after work.

I had to buy my uniform; I wore white, like a nurse. The Food Building was warm and I brought other clothes with me, too, to change into when I finished working. They didn't have polyester like they have nowadays, and I took my uniform home every night, washed it, starched it, and hung it up. In the morning I'd dampen and iron it, put it on, and go to work. I wasn't about to buy another uniform because wages were very low at that time. In fact, in my previous job I worked for $16 a week for a 13-hour day. It was a split shift, and I had a glorious Monday as my day off.

I was boy crazy most of the time, so I was always interested in whatever date was going to come along. After work everybody went to listen to big bands and to dance. I'm not as fond of the big bands now as I was then. It was the music of the times, I was of the times, and I enjoyed it then. My husband also worked at the Fair, but we didn't meet until later.

Everybody liked the fountains; they were so beautiful. And the lighting was beautiful. When we took the ferry home at night we'd look back to see the buildings illuminated.

I would travel on the ferry with other people who worked there. I was friendly with some of the people

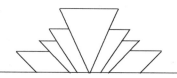

who worked at the Gayway. One of them was a sword-swallower, and he kind of taught me how to swallow a sword. I practiced a little bit when I got home, but I kept gagging, so I gave up.

Also, I met a man who ate glass. He told me he would eat a lot of bread before eating the glass. He would rinse his mouth out with alum, or something like that, which closed the pores up, and then he would start to chew the glass. He began with thin glass, like light bulbs, chewing it with other things, like soft bread and potatoes, and things like that. The mucous membranes are very tough, much more than people realize, and I think once the glass got past a certain point it got carried right on down. You can get into

> *One piece would stick to another, and pretty soon I had great big caramel corn feet.*

trouble, though, if it sticks into something on the way. I wouldn't recommend trying this! This man also swallowed a lit neon tube which you could see glowing through his stomach.

And I used to know the Fat Lady. She wasn't a friendly person. I would speak to her, but she just sort of sat quietly in the corner. I used to feel very sorry for her. I think she weighed more than 500 pounds.

Then there was the Bearded Lady. I think it was a real beard. It was a puzzle to me.

I was fascinated by Esther Williams; I thought she was wonderful. I'm not impressed too much by personalities in entertainment, but I loved the Aquacade. I think that was my favorite show.

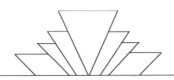

ERNEST BRYMER

My part in the Fair was, I think, very small. I went to work there in the late summer of '39 as a rolling chairboy. I guess I was about 20. I recall my first job after high school was working for a bakery equipment company repairing the equipment. I was still looking around, and I had no idea what I wanted to do, except I knew I wanted to be a millionaire.

I loved the Fair. I think it was one of the most wonderful times of my life. When I wasn't pushing people around, I was just sitting in the Pacifica area looking at the statue and the lights.

We used to rent the rolling chairs daily. Sometimes there would be no chairs; other times there would be hundreds. It was strictly your own thing. You just paid a set amount for the chair, and you could make it back very quickly. There were two shifts. I would always rent in the latter half of the morning for both shifts and work right on through until darkness because I liked it so much.

There was a standard fee we charged, but there was a lot of leeway. Sometimes people would just want to go to a certain building. I would always tell them it was a dollar minimum. If we got there in five minutes, it worked very well for me. Other times you would get people who would want more than a ride from place to place. They would want to see things, want to tour, want a little conversation. In those instances you would make your own price.

Most people tipped. I strove to make the amount uneven, like $1.50 or $2.50, so if they gave me $2.00 or $3.00 they might leave the rest for the tip. Probably the best tip I got was $15. Four gentlemen from Coca Cola had been to some kind of a meeting, and they wanted to get a good view of the Fair. They happened to get in my chair and in another fellow's and we took them all around to everything. They were primarily interested in the Gayway and in the bars. We ended up at the Philippine Bar. We could roll our chairs right

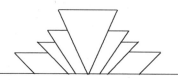

in. It was sort of a bamboo structure and it had a little ramp. A few of us would make kind of an act of pushing the chairs into the bar, and the customers could sit right there and have their drinks. This worked out well that evening. At the end of the ride they gave us each a $15 tip. We were both shocked and happy. In fact we ran for five or ten minutes so they wouldn't reconsider.

Some people would come to the parking lot with a chauffeur; you would rush right up to that car. It was surprising how many elderly ladies would come that way and would have robes to put on their laps. It was definitely a luxury; unless you were well-to-do it was expensive to have a chair pusher.

I don't recall any famous people getting into my chair. The ride that stands out is one where I took three of the girls from Sally Rand's Nude Ranch and pushed them through the Gayway as an advertising stunt. They were hanging on the chair and jumping off and on to get attention. They had on little leather cowgirl outfits, as I recall, with cowgirl hats. They exposed a good deal of flesh during that ride.

After work I stayed and enjoyed the Fair. I will say it was there that I was more or less introduced to the zombie, a drink which was the specialty of the Philippine Bar. I made some friends in the group of rolling chairboys, and we'd go after work and have a zombie. They claimed that a person could drink only one, but of course we always tried to drink more. Oddly enough, I very seldom took a date to the Fair. Maybe three or four times. It was my place of work. And at that time there were a lot of things to do in San Francisco, so I usually dated there. Although my wife was working at the Fair, we didn't know each other then.

When the Fair closed I started in electrical sales, and I kept on in that until I worked for General Electric Supply Company as a salesman. And then I left that job and for 20 years had my own business — electrical contracting.

> *A few of us would make kind of an act of pushing the chairs into the bar, and the customers would sit right there and have their drinks.*

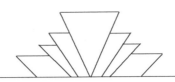

BILL HARRIS

I was born in Canada in 1916 and came to the Bay Area during the Depression on a freight train.

I went to work and attended night school at the University of California Extension on Powell and Sutter Streets. From there I went to work at Bethlehem Steel, but during the Fair I took time off to work on Treasure Island. At Bethlehem Steel I was making only about $25 a week, and at the Fair I made $300-$400 a month. The Fair was the place to be.

I was hired as a regular chairboy. On the third day Mr. McPherson, the manager for Mr. Walgreen, who owned the concession, looked like he needed some help. You got to figure 300 kids were there to push chairs and that took organization. So I went to him and he said, "Do you want to give me a hand?" I said, "Certainly." So that's how it all happened. In a couple of days he asked, "Would you be interested in taking the bike and riding around the grounds from noon until 5 p.m. to see what help is needed with the chairboys? Then you could push the chair yourself from 5

Bill Harris, a Bay Area businessman, took a leave from his job at Bethlehem Steel Company to be a rolling chair supervisor at the Fair.

p.m. until as late as you like." I thought that was a pretty good set up.

Rolling chairs are good for old timers. Being an old timer myself now I can appreciate them. It was a long hike from the parking lot to the Fair, so that was a good place to get customers. Once you got them in the chair, you could say that you could show them the Fair in two to six hours. A lot of visitors would just sit in the chair all day and at lunchtime take the chairboy with them for lunch. Ever since then, at every fair my wife and I have visited — Seattle in '62, New York in '64, and Montreal in '67 — we've always gotten a chair to take us around.

So at Treasure Island during the daytime I ran around on a bicycle. If there were any problems, if some of the chairboys couldn't collect, I was there to see that they collected. There wasn't too much trouble. Sometimes some of our boys wouldn't be polite to their

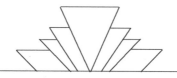

customers, so it would really be their fault if they couldn't collect. We kind of watched, and if we found anyone was rude to the customers, we would let him go. As soon as one would leave we could put another one right on. Lots of college boys wanted that job.

One of the unusual things for this area where it virtually never snows was the ski jump. It wasn't successful and lasted only a couple of weeks. The homemade snow they made then wasn't as good as the kind they make now. But I remember taking people to see it.

Many people forget the Livestock Pavilion on the Fairgrounds. Besides livestock shows, they used the auditorium there for horse shows, opera singing, and prize fights. As a matter of fact I entered into one of the fights there, a heavyweight. I won the prize for most popular fighter, but I was TKO'd in the third round. We found out later that someone had doped me. And I remember Lily Pons used the Livestock Pavilion for a week for her show.

Wallace Beery was one of my memorable rolling chair customers. After I had pushed him around for awhile, he got up and said, "Now, kid, I'll push you." Judy Garland was one of my customers. She was only about 17 years old then, a beautiful thing. Some of the boys told me when they had Bing Crosby, he would walk as others in his party rode in the chairs.

One of the chairboys used to date Esther Williams who was swimming at the Aquacade there. He married another girl from the Fair and now lives in Walnut Creek. He was from Texas, and like a lot of boys, he stayed out here.

Johnny Weissmuller, who also swam at the

> *I was TKO'd in the third round. We found out later that someone had doped me.*

Aquacade, had his yacht parked in the marina, close to where the DC 3 Pan-American Clipper came in. A few of us got to know Weissmuller, and when he wasn't gallivanting on his yacht, he let us stay there.

After the Fair I returned to Bethlehem, and stayed in the ship repair and ship maintenance business. I worked for Kaiser and was in ship building during the war. After that I went into business for myself.

H&H Ship Service is the name of my company. We're really an environmental company now. My repair company is J&H Marine and Engineering Company, and my recycling company is Brisbane Recycling. If you look towards Brisbane over to the right going to the airport you'll see where there is a big pile of dirt there. That's my dirt — my gold. Concrete that has been torn up from roads and buildings is hauled to me in Brisbane. I take all class-3 materials of concrete. It has steel in it. I've put a crushing plant there and a big magnet to pull the steel out as we crush the concrete, and then I sell it back to the contractors for road base. I got the idea thirteen years ago, and it took me six years to sell this idea to the public. I had an engineer (one of the old chairboys) come out from Vietnam, and I backed him while he started the business. He died soon afterwards, so I had to take it over. Now we have a good thing going.

I still am friends with some other rolling chairboys. One now lives in Dallas, one in Houston, and one in New York. There are about seven or eight of us right here in this area. I always look forward to the reunions. One time my wife and I had about 25 chairboys come to our house for a party. I like keeping in touch.

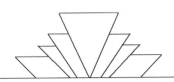

LUCILLE CROSBY

I must have been 20 in 1939 and I was working in an employment office in San Francisco. Now I can't even remember the name of the office. I gave typing tests, and I used to see jobs come through. One day I went to my boss and said, "Gee, I'd like to go work at the Fair." "You're not the type," she said. "They want somebody that's real outgoing. You're too shy." "Let me try it," I said. "I can't stand this click-click-click anymore." So she finally saw I really meant it, and she said, "OK. You've got a job there."

It was a popcorn stand, a big, covered stand where you made popcorn and had three big rings of mixed nuts and such that went around and were warm, and on the other side a bunch of Hershey bars, all at this one stand.

At first I worked at a stand right behind the Folies Bergère. The dancers, producers, and such of the Folies would come over and buy a candy bar or peanuts, but there wasn't much traffic at that stand. But the Elephant Trains would come by every 20 minutes

and that was always something to look forward to. Ted was driving an Elephant Train and he'd come by and stop at the stand. "On the right is the Folies Bergère," he'd say, "and on the left is Lucille's popcorn stand." Then he'd get out and steal my candy bars and give them to all the people. I'd have to get out of the stand and collect a nickel from everybody. Oh, I hated him! I'd take a broom after him! But it was fun.

We worked seven days a week, 12, 15, or 16 hours a day. If you didn't, why there was somebody right behind you who would. It was your life. You stayed there and you worked, and when you went home, it was just to sleep. Then you'd get up and go to work. Period.

Doing popcorn itself wasn't that interesting, but there were different faces all the time. Since I worked at the stand I didn't have to pay for that food, and the

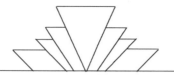
same people owned hot dog stands, so I got all my food free. Mike Shapiro was my boss. Oh, I remember Mike. We went round and round, he and I, many times. He was a good guy. He used to come around to the stand, and he'd say, "OK, Lou, you can have 15 minutes off. Get yourself a hamburger or something." And I'd say, "Well, get in here. I have to go to the bathroom!"

> *"On the right is the Folies Bergère," he'd say, "and on the left is Lucille's popcorn stand."*

A lot of the people working at the Fair would knock-down. I never did. They had spotters there who would watch to see if you were knocking-down. Two for me, one for the company. So, one day Mike came by and said I was knocking-down. So I said, "Mike, I'm not. I've never taken a penny from this thing, and I don't intend to." So he left. The more I thought of it the madder I got. So I finally closed the stand. It took about half an hour to close. I had to turn off all the machines, put up all the boards, and lock the whole thing up.

This was about two o'clock in the afternoon. Then I ran over to the office and Mike was sitting there. "My God, Lucille, what are you doing here?" "You can take your God damn job! I'm not knocking-down and I have never knocked-down on the stand!" I went into the ladies' room, slammed the door and changed my clothes. We had little yellow pirate-like uniforms. All the time I was changing, Mike was yelling, "Lou, it was a mistake. It wasn't you. I'm sorry." So when I was all dressed, I came out and he said, "You go and get yourself something to eat and something to drink and settle down. You can have the rest of the day off. Come back tomorrow and everything will be all right." I was still as mad as could be, so I said, "I'm not going to work for you anymore. I don't even like that stand!" That was something for me, because at that time I was really pretty shy. Anyway, I did go back, and he put me on another stand where I wanted to be. But I was pretty scared when I quit so dramatically because there were lots of people for every job. This was 1939, remember.

Then instead of being by the Folies, I was up at the terminal. There was something going on there all the time. The boats came in there and you'd see all the people coming and going or waiting for boats. That's where the Elephant Trains started, and they had a big elephant there part of the time. My mother took a picture of me standing by that great big elephant. I was scared to death.

There were lots of young people working at the Fair, but all the girls liked the Key System guys. A lot of them were in college, or junior college, and they were guys who wanted to go someplace and do something with their lives. They weren't just satisfied selling peanuts.

Ted used to come over to the stand, and we'd get to talking. He was so cute. He was really nice, too. Really nice. I remember they were going to have an Elephant Train dance. Boy, all the girls at the Fair wanted to go to that dance. That's all there was to it. You were nobody if you didn't get to go to that dance. So I thought, "Oh, shoot. I have to go to that dance somehow." So I asked Ted. He couldn't dance at all then. He can't dance now, but at that time he really couldn't. But he said he'd take me. After that all the kids seemed to put us together. If they saw Ted they'd say, "Where's Lou?" Or to me, "Where's Ted?"

The Fair was the most beautiful, romantic place in the world. The lighting, the flowers, the way it was presented, everything. It was like a fantasy land. Sometimes it was cold and rainy, yes, I'll grant you that, but everyone was so friendly.

At about 10:30 every night the exhibits would close and the older people and the families would go home. We'd be finished for the night and that's when we'd go to the dances. The Gayway would stay open, and sometimes we'd go there. I saw Gyspy Rose Lee at the Gayway. She was very nice. I thought her show was very daring, but you couldn't see a damn thing. But this was 1939, you know. If she did the same thing now she wouldn't be daring at all.

The night the Fair closed we all cried. Everybody did. They played "taps" and turned out the lights, sort of one by one, and I just cried. And it was so quiet. And then the whole Fair went black.

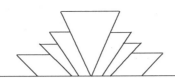

TED CROSBY

The Key System had hired George and Herman Markley to run the transportation at the Fair. The Markleys had worked the 1933 Chicago Fair, so they were a natural. I had just gotten out of high school and this ad was in the paper and one of my buddies called and said, "Let's go down and see what it's all about." I went to work the next day, right out of high school.

I went over to drive the Elephant Trains. The trains had a '39 Ford 3/4 ton pick-up chassis that they converted to an elephant shape. Our terminal was near the two Elephant Towers, and even when the trains were parked, people would get up into them and just sit. After the Fair they were sold-off by the Key System to parks and scattered all over the place.

We never had any accidents. The second and third sections had wheels on the rear only, and each section sat on the one in the front of it. As you would turn corners, the sections tended to cut in, and we would have people who got caught with the sections cutting in. We watched carefully and would try to alert anyone in the way, but some people just wouldn't move.

Sometimes we'd have foreign visitors. They would have their own interpreters. At that time we were getting a little touchy with Japan, so we didn't have any Japanese tourists like we have today.

We normally worked about 12 hours a day, but on the big holidays, you know, Washington's Birthday, Labor Day, that type of thing, they wanted to keep all the trains going that they could. So many of those days I'd work from 7:30 in the morning until midnight or one o'clock. Our hourly wage was 42 cents. When most of the Fair closed down in the evenings, that's when we'd break away from what we were doing and we would go to where the bands were playing. All of them were there one time or another, Count Basie, Jimmy

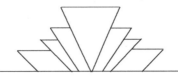

Dorsey, Tommy Dorsey, Kay Kyser.

Everybody was jitterbugging then. I wasn't that good at it, but Lou was. She took a number of prizes with other people. They would actually run jitterbugging contests over there. I have two left feet, and can't carry a tune in a wheelbarrow, but I would like to get out there to the slower tunes. No one wanted the dances to end. They'd announce, "We're going to close. This is the last dance. The last ferry's about to leave." People would clap and say, "Keep playing." The Key System also serviced the Fair with buses and you could catch a bus later than the last ferry.

Sometimes we'd get stuck overnight. I remember one time when I drove over, Lou and I went into the parking lot after one of the dances. When we got into the car I said, "Let's just rest a minute. I'm beat." Lou was too, and we fell asleep sitting there. We just slept there all night long. We were so worn out we didn't wake up until morning when people were arriving and the sun was coming up. We wore uniforms and had a locker room and showers, so after cleaning up we went right back to work.

Lou and I continued to see each other, and then, when I was about to join the Navy in '42, we went to Reno and got married. I was afraid she'd be gone if we waited until after the war. That's 46 years ago.

At the end of the Fair the Key System put out a book, like a high school yearbook, with everyone's picture and address. They called me "Midget" because I'm smaller than the average guy. I'm 5'6", but for the picture they put me on a box and teamed me up with a fellow who was 6'6" for the fun of it. We were all good friends, like one happy family.

Some other people we associated with were the rolling chairboys. People would take our trip around the grounds, and if they were elderly, they would say, "Is there another way to get around?" And we'd say, "Yeah, there sure is—the rolling chairs." Most of the rolling chair boys had a good lecture worked up and knew all the different exhibits. We would get to know them, and we'd have our favorites. When we'd find a

> *He'd go up there and stall out and spin that sucker... and then he'd go under the bridge.*

person who wanted to do that, we'd say, "Hey, stay on the train until I find you a good one." Pretty soon we'd spot a friend, and if he didn't have a fare, we'd whistle him over, stop the train and get him a fare. The boys were always around huckstering.

I used to stop the train, too, whenever the stunt plane was in the air. I always was going to fly myself, one way or another, and there was this pilot named Turner. He'd get up there in a little bi-plane and do acrobatics. I'd stop the Elephant Train and tell the people, "Hey, you gotta wait. We have to watch this." He put on just an excellent show. Precision stuff. He'd go up there and stall out and spin that sucker. He would come down and recover just above the water, and then he'd go under the bridge. I was impressed.

There were other things to see. We didn't have much time, but the Cavalcade was a great show with horses and trains and Indian fights. Randolph Scott was one of the guys in that who headed up some wagon train stuff. The Aquacade had Johnny Weissmuller swinging out of the overhead on a rope, like Tarzan, and then diving into the water before doing a few laps.

The Folies was the true Folies Bergère. It was spectacular. I can tell you about Sally Rand and the Nude Ranch. By today's standards it wasn't much. The girls had cowboy hats and a gun belt. Their breasts were exposed, but that's about all. A sheet of glass separated the public from the girls. You went in one door and progressed through. It wasn't a show you went in and sat down for. You just went through and out again.

I would never have gone to college if it weren't for that Fair. I wanted to go to school but just didn't have the finances until I worked there. Abbot, my high school friend who went with me to apply for the job, was a good athlete. He had signed with Marin Junior College on an athletic scholarship. He suggested I join him over there, and that's how I got started in college. I started after the Fair closed the first year, but I was glad to go back for the second year of the Fair. Then I had enough money for Marin and Cal.

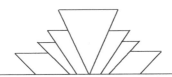

CHARLES DOUGHERTY

We had an assemblyman from down the Peninsula who was on the Exposition Board. I asked him about working at the Fair, and he referred me to the retired sergeant major who was in charge of the civilian guards. That's how I found my job at the Fair. It might have helped that I knew Police Chief Dullea.

The guards weren't police officers, but we wore uniforms and had badges which said "Special Officer for San Francisco." We couldn't arrest anyone. Our jobs were more or less to keep traffic moving, to keep cars from coming in the areas where they weren't allowed, and to see that plants weren't stolen. We wore blue jackets, yellow pants with blue stripes down the sides, yellow belts and blue caps with black visors.

We did carry guns, but I carried the bullets in my pocket. I wasn't looking for any trouble. San Francisco uniformed police and detectives were there, and trouble was their job. Our job was to walk around.

For the longest time I was stationed on the road

Charles Dougherty, a steward at Bay Meadows and Golden Gate Fields, worked as a guard at the Fair while he was attending San Mateo Junior College.

behind the Women's Club to turn people away from driving to the back entrance of the Aquacade. At the ferry landing people would rush to get off or on the ferries, and we kept them moving to avoid congestion at the gates. Another spot was the Gayway. People would try to get into concessions without paying.

One of the things to watch each evening was the lowering of the flag. A detachment from the U.S. Army that lived right on the Island, a ceremonial outfit, performed that duty. We'd have to keep the crowds back when they marched.

I used to draw the 4 p.m. to midnight shift. That was a good time for music. I remember enjoying the San Francisco Municipal Band, and the San Francisco Symphony. I'll never forget, one night Oscar Levant was playing with the Symphony and he kept bouncing up and down. During the intermission I was back-

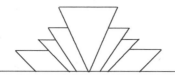

stage and heard someone say, "Oscar, I've never seen you play that style before." He said, "I have a boil on my backside, and I can't sit too long."

When they had big-name bands there, it was nice to draw duty in the ballroom. There were always pretty girls there, not only visitors, but sometimes girls from the Aquacade or the Folies Bergère would be there. A lot of the girls who worked on the Island stayed at the Broadmoor Hotel on Sutter Street. I remember parties there. Back then you weren't afraid to go around San Francisco. You weren't afraid of getting mugged or held up.

The people who worked at the Fair had a good esprit de corps. If a friend was going to the Aquacade we'd tell him to say to the guard, "My name is Flynn." Then the guard would say, "You're in." Or if we didn't like a guy, we'd tell him to say, "My name is Stout," and then the guard would say, "Then you're out."

Once in a while you'd hear what happened to some of the fellows. Ham Pool played and coached for the L.A. Rams, Bob Cleckner became the assistant

> *We did carry guns, but I carried the bullets in my pocket.*

coach and trainer for U.S.F. and the 49ers. One of the Aquacade swimmers, Harry Griswold, I think, invented the trampoline. He used it in his diving act. Another swimmer, Clyde Devine, was an all-American at Oregon State. Duane Carmody became a career Naval Officer and retired as Vice Admiral.

One thing, I think, that saved the Fair was the Aquacade. It was an hour-and-a-half show, with diving and swimming and beautiful show girls. That was the first time I had ever seen synchronized swimming. Morton Downey, a tenor from Ireland, sang at the show. He always had one or two priests around him. Johnny Weissmuller was a nice guy after he got to know you. Esther Williams had an infectious smile and always was an enthusiastic conversationalist.

Being a guard at the Fair was a great summer job. We made $125 a month. A lot of fellows wearing Hastings suits and Bostonian shoes on Montgomery Street weren't making that kind of money. And I took pride in helping people find their way, and in answering questions. I was proud to work there.

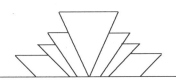

JAMES GREALISH

My recollection is going over to the Fair as a kid of 19 with a couple of bucks to see the shows. The main attraction for kids my age was not so much the exhibits, but the dancing. It was a big deal to go across the Bay and have a night over there, listening to Benny Goodman or whoever it might be. It wasn't very expensive in those days. That was a typical college or high school approach to the Fair. I was shy, I guess. There were always plenty of girls. We'd get courage in numbers. Sometimes I'd take a date.

You could go over by ferry or by train. When the Bridge was built, traffic went both ways on the upper deck. The lower deck was used by trains and trucks. The trains stopped at a station on Treasure Island.

When the Fair opened, the fire protection was provided by the San Francisco Fire Department.

Rear Admiral James Grealish visited the Fair while a college student. He later went on to head the Naval Reserve Readiness Command on Treasure Island.

Later it was protected by the Federal Fire Department. They had a big banquet at the fire house once during the Fair. A couple of friends and I went over and washed all the dishes and cleaned up after the banquet for five bucks apiece.

One of the fellows who worked as a janitor, and who was going to San Jose State at the time, Martin Carmody, went in the Navy and became a pilot. He eventually became an admiral and was the Commandant of the 122th Naval District. His office was upstairs from mine before I retired in 1978 in what had been the Fair's Administration Building. He had worked as a janitor in the same building over there in the summer of '39.

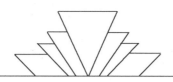

CARL HEYNEN

I used to go over to Treasure Island while the Fair buildings were being constructed. I was going with a girl who had a job as a secretary to one of the architects who designed buildings on the fairgrounds. I went over with her occasionally when she had to check work on the Island. It was a real busy place. They tried to build it in a hurry. Many of the things, like the Tower of the Sun, were just shells, stucco on the outside. They were very pretty but very fragile.

Even though it was built quickly, the Fair was a finished project when it opened. I went over occasionally to walk around, see exhibits, and listen to the big bands. It was glamorous.

The war was not on my mind even though I was in the Navy. The war was going on in Europe, but it wasn't touching us out here. We never thought much about it until Pearl Harbor.

I remember getting a telephone call on a Monday night about 8:30 p.m. to report for active duty Wednesday at 8 a.m. I was sent to Yerba Buena Island where *The Delta Queen* was berthed. It was a river boat that had gone for years from Sacramento to San Francisco and back again. We used it as a barracks while TI was being readied for the Navy. The first few days they still had the civilian crew working on *The Delta Queen*, serving us steaks, using cloth napkins and tablecloths, just like we were on a cruise. That soon ended when our own Navy crew took over.

We were the first of the US Navy on Treasure Island. There were about 300 of us from the First, Second, Third, Fourth, Fifth, and Sixth Divisions of the Naval Reserve from the San Francisco Bay and Santa Cruz areas. The Fair buildings were leveled and barracks were built on the Island while some of us stayed in Tiburon and others stayed on *The Delta King* and *Queen*, identical sister stern wheel river boats.

I saw the destruction of the Fair buildings. The

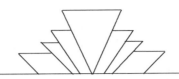

CARL HEYNEN

Navy took balls, cranes and bulldozers, pushed the buildings down, scraped them up, and hauled them away. I used to walk around, and I would think about how beautiful it used to be during the Fair.

Governor Olson opened the Fair with the official key, a beautiful thing said to be valued at $35,000. Jewelers from all over the state donated stones and gold for it to be made. After the Fair closed, the key was raffled or auctioned off to those jewelers and the one who won it put it in his home and it was lost for many years. No one knew where it was. When the jeweler died, his daughter got it and brought it to sell

> *The Navy took balls, cranes and bulldozers, pushed the buildings down, scraped them up, and hauled them away.*

to the museum at Treasure Island. Ernest Steen, James Nicholson, Zoe Dell Lantis Nutter, and I donated money to buy it for the museum, and it will someday be put on display there.

I was glad to have been able to help buy the key for the museum. Treasure Island is like my second home. I was there when it was being built, then during the Fair, and also when the Navy first took it over to establish a naval station. I still spend a lot of time over there, working on the reunions of the first Navy men on the Island, as a member of the Board of Directors of the museum, and as a member of the Board of Directors of the Navy League.

MICHAEL F. CROWE

There was an emphasis on the Pacific Basin at the time the Fair at Treasure Island was being constructed. The Pacific Rim was going to be opened for exploitation, and San Francisco and the Bay Area wanted to be the center for that. So some of the buildings were designed at the Fair to recall the Pacific Basin. But when you look at them in their detailing, many are really Art Deco, the style that flourished from 1925 until the out break of the Second World War. It was influenced by the invention of new materials, such as neon, Bakelite, Formica, those kinds of things.

The 1925 Paris Exhibition, where Art Deco gets its name, allowed exhibitors to show products only of modern design. At that time the U.S. Chamber of Commerce, headed by Herbert Hoover, said the U.S. would not have a pavilion because we had no modern art and we didn't know what it was. Instead he sent a committee to attend the Exposition, and when they came back, they prepared a travelling exhibit that went to all major museums. Then the major depart-

Michael F. Crowe is an architectural historian for the National Park Service and Founder and President of the Art Deco Society of California.

ment stores, like Lord and Taylor and Bloomingdales, organized display to show people what was going on in European design. That's when Art Deco really got off the ground in this country, in 1926.

The movies were an important vehicle in promoting Art Deco. Stars like Gloria Swanson were very sophisticated in terms of what was going on in European design and actually brought European architects back to Hollywood to design movie sets. Then people began to hire those architects to re-design their homes, or design new ones.

Very standard Art Deco elements found at the Fair in the buildings and in the decorations are zigzags, steps, rays, chevrons, and stylized flowers. Flowers were shown as single round circles surrounded by scalloped edges, very flat, very two-dimensional. The Mayan influence can also be seen in the Fair decora-

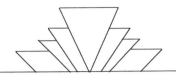

tions. There was a very strong Egyptian revival after 1922, and a lot of those kinds of style elements were also used.

There is a misconception that Art Deco is always pastel. For the most part there is a strong use of color in Art Deco. This was very much a part of the lighting of the Fair buildings. The idea of using strong color on buildings, not only to paint them but also to light them, was something that was an outgrowth of German Expressionism. German Expressionist architects had called for large crystal constructions at the tops of mountains that would be lit from the inside, so that it would look as if the mountains were glowing at night. Indirect lighting was used at the Paris Exposition of 1925. So it was not unusual to find it at the 1939-1940 Exposition. The lights there were hidden in the bushes and trees. Naked light bulbs were not considered attractive anymore. At one time they had been, of course; they were considered wonderful because they were a new invention, so you wanted to see them, to show them off. But by 1939 the movement was to control them a little—create moods.

Not all of the Fair buildings were Art Deco. The Federal Building on the Island took the Bauhaus approach. The Bauhaus was a school founded in Germany in the late 1920s continuing to the early 1930s, when it was disbanded by Hitler. Bauhaus architects felt there should be absolutely no ornament on a building, that the beauty of a building is best expressed in terms of proportions, rich materials, and an

> *There is a misconception that Art Deco is always pastel. For the most part there is a strong use of color in Art Deco.*

attention to craftsmanship in details. There is a suggestion of decoration in the Federal Building, but for the most part it has the stripped-down look.

Some of the buildings, even if they recalled certain styles of architecture, defied categorization. You also have to look at what was happening in San Francisco. Some elements at the Fair were very similar to the facade of the Royal Theater on Polk Street, designed by Timothy Pfleuger.

Murals were very much a part of this period. The most famous one done at the Fair was the Diego Rivera mural, which is now at City College. It was a sort of culmination for Rivera to come back to the city that launched his career in this country. Almost ten years before, he had done the mural at the Stock Exchange Club in San Francisco. It was quite an ordeal because he was an avowed communist and the immigration service prevented him from entering this country for a full year. Then from San Francisco he went to New York to do the murals at Radio City Music Hall, and from there he went to Detroit. To come back to do a mural on Treasure Island must have been quite exciting for him. He also provided inspiration and training for local artists. I'm thinking of the Bruton Sisters who did murals on Treasure Island and also at the Fairmont Hotel.

It is unfortunate, but very typical that the temporary buildings were town down. tearing them down was very typical. Very few buildings from expositions have ever been preserved.

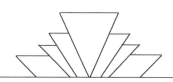

LYLE BRAMSON

The Fair was a very important part of my life, and it still is. As an employee, part of the Revenue Service Department, I had different responsibilities. I was concerned with hiring and training the employees. Whenever money was collected at the Fair, I had to see that it was safely deposited. Our department issued passes to the VIPs.

In 1939 there was a lot of unemployment. We started to hire people about eight weeks before the opening of the Fair, and every time we put the word out, 30 to 50 people at a time would apply. We started with about 1200 people, a crew for everything. Maintenance, publicity, cashiers, rolling chair guides, everything. Attendance, especially during the weekdays, was not as high as we expected, so unfortunately, we had to let many employees go.

We had a lot of students who could just work weekends, so that fit our needs quite well. All the colleges, especially Cal, furnished students. They made real good public relations people because they really

Lyle Bramson is President of the Association of Retired Employees of the Fair at Treasure Island, and as such is responsible for yearly reunions.

got with it. As guides they were taught that if anyone asked a question in a serious manner or frame of mind, it would not be a foolish question. One lady wanted to know if we were going to tear down the bridges when the Fair was over. Another lady very seriously asked, "What time do they feed the lagoons?"

Starting even in the early part of the Fair a lot of San Francisco families, especially the Jewish families, and even corporations would sponsor kids from Europe. They would ask us to take them as employees. We called them refugees. They were smart kids, but they were fearful because their homeland was being kicked around by the Nazi machine. Some of the kids didn't speak English and we would dig and dig for something that they could do. In the accounting room we had an area where the stubs of the tickets that were picked up had to match the cashier's report for that

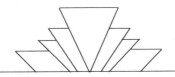

particular entry or show. These kids had the drudgery of sitting there and sorting stubs, separating the children's and the adults' stubs, counting them, and then making a report. That didn't require the English language, but they learned very rapidly. In about a month we could put them out to do almost anything.

The average age of the employees was in the 20s someplace. We would get so weary by the end of the day that we could just barely get to the ferry to get home. We were younger then, and we would snap right back and come back the next day.

We were officially known as the Revenue Control Department. The Exposition sponsored events, be it a public dance, or another gathering, where they charged admission and it would be my job to take care of the revenue. The cashier's division would send me a number of cashiers who would work the necessary hours, and I would call the guard division for security. Where money was concerned, I was concerned.

Everyone came to the Fair. It was our department that met the celebrities and gave them passes. Most of the exhibits were free once you paid your admission to the fairgrounds. But some things would cost 10 cents or 25 cents, something like that. With the passes a person could go anywhere for free.

We had all the entertainers, Jack Benny, Edgar Bergen, Judy Garland. The Lark was the train that ran from Los Angeles. The movie stars appearing at the Fair would ride all night in the train and we would put them up at the St. Francis Hotel. They would play gin rummy all night on the train, so when they arrived they would go to the hotel and go to bed. But they were due over at the Fair when they got off the train, so we would have to go over and shake them out of the hotel.

Sometimes I would escort them around the Fair, but usually I just gave them passes. I fondly remember escorting Madeline Carroll around the grounds. That was a fine day for me because she was a beautiful lady.

There was a world famous gate-crasher around that time, One-eyed O'Connelly, and sure enough, he got in without a ticket or pass. It was a publicity stunt, I believe. He was notorious for getting in anywhere.

> *Another lady very seriously asked, "What time do they feed the lagoons?"*

Every orchestra that travelled played at the Fair. Benny Goodman was there for 30 days, and we had the Dorseys, Phil Harris, Count Basie, Kay Kyser. Different companies would sponsor some of the stars. Grace Moore was there for IBM Day and Bing Crosby for Safeway Day. Johnny Weissmuller and Esther Williams were the stars of Billy Rose's Aquacade. Johnny was quiet, very, very quiet. Esther Williams was just a teenager, newly married at that time to a doctor. She would often arrive late by cab. I remember Betty Grable and Roddy McDowell were both very young then, too, and they would come with their mothers.

Radio played a big part with the celebrities. ABC was just new, and NBC Blue Network and NBC Red Network were at the Fair. They furnished the Fair announcers, and had the finest PA system. That's old hat now, but a PA system was new at that time. The announcers had familiar, tremendous voices. It wasn't a place where visitors were boomed at, but when there was an announcement, everyone heard it. We had Ira Blue, of course, Art Linkletter and Mel Venter.

Art Linkletter probably got his start emceeing at the Cavalcade. We had the largest outdoor stage that had ever existed for that show. We could put two train engines and probably 100 horses and 250 people on that stage at one time.

We had a lot of cooperation from the newspapers. Somewhere on the front page each day they would print the highlights. Herb Caen was a cub writer fresh from Sacramento, and I remember, he always wore a heavy sweater with leather patches on the elbows. He would come to our office and say, "What's happened that I should know about?" He was a very endearing, solicitous guy at that time.

There were two groups of employees, the Promotion Committee, which has had reunions ever since the end of the war, and our group of former employees. We call ourselves "The Royal Order of Cashiers." The two groups joined together around 1958 and at first had dinner meetings, with guest speakers. Now every February 18th, on the anniversary of Opening Day, we have a luncheon with usually about 70 people, some-

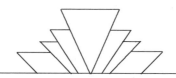

times as many as 150 attending.

For the 20th Anniversary of the Fair the Navy opened Treasure Island to the public, and what a day that was! The shore patrol was just overwhelmed by the great numbers of people who came to see what they could, remembering the good times they had had. My wife and I had met at the Fair. She worked in the part of Revenue Control which prepared the passes. We had always thought that our meeting there and marrying was rather an exclusive thing. But on the day of the 20th Anniversary, we found any number of people who had met their spouses there.

Pretty soon it will be time for the 50th Anniversary. Ted Huggins, a retired Standard Oil man, was responsible for getting enthusiasm rolling for a Fair in the first place, for an island to celebrate the bridges, and so many other aspects of the Fair. He was the one who arranged for the 20th celebration. He is not well now, and his help will be sorely missed in planning for

> *They were very smart kids, but they were fearful because their homeland was being kicked to pieces by the Nazi machine.*

the 50th. But we will do something special!

Eventually I would like to see a park area where the parking lot is now, in front of the former Administration Building. That area now houses both a Navy Museum and a museum of Fair memorabilia. Perhaps in the little park we could have plaques commemorating the Fair, or maybe a bust of Ted Huggins, and one of Marshall Dill, the President of the second year. There's a plan to move the remaining parts of one of the fountains to that area. That would be nice, but it costs a lot of money to do that. Well, we'll just have to see.

What we lack in money our association makes up for in enthusiasm. People come to the reunion luncheons on walkers and in wheelchairs. But they do like to talk about Treasure Island! The restaurant has to almost throw us out at the end of the day. Oh yes, Treasure Island was quite a place. It has a very solid place in many lives.

AL CLEARY

My father, Alfred J. Cleary, was just one heck of a good guy. He was well-educated and smart as a whip. He graduated from St. Ignatius and then went on to graduate from the University of California at Berkeley as a civil engineer. He was actively involved in most engineering projects in Northern California and served as Chief Assistant City Engineer of San Francisco in charge of the Hetch Hetchy project. As consulting engineer for the State of California he helped select the site for the Bay Bridge.

In 1932 my father was appointed the first Chief Administrative Officer of San Francisco by Mayor Angelo Rossi. It was a lifetime appointment; he served only nine years before he died suddenly in 1941. He was a great public relations man and the mayor used to ask him to represent the city at most civic affairs. The mayor also appointed him as the city's representative on the Golden Gate International Exposition Board. Although Leland Cutler was president of the Exposition the first year and Marshall Dill the second

> *Al Cleary's father was the city's Chief Administrative Officer at the time of the Fair. Al worked there as a guide and later owned Clementina Construction Company.*

year, my father oversaw the entire Fair.

Most San Franciscans were enthusiastic about the Exposition, but I remember that many worried about competing with New York, which had a World's Fair the same year. Since permission had been granted to pump the sand and build the island, the administration decided to go ahead with the project, and they pursued a plan of cooperation with New York. Mayor Rossi and my father met many times with Mayor La Guardia of New York to iron out any competition problems.

The political climate in those days was different from what it is today. The 1929 crash and Depression that followed was not far in the past. The citizens had worries other than what elected officials were doing. It seemed as if the voters elected their officials and then placed their confidence and trust in them. The administration did not have to go out and sell the community

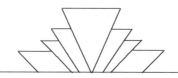

on the Exposition. There were few, if any, formal opposition groups.

The plan was to have an exposition that the City could be proud of and also not be a financial disaster. Everyone felt it must be a first-class operation and good for San Francisco. I don't remember anyone mentioning "good for the Bay Area." In those days San Francisco was more insular than it is today.

The Exposition lost money the first year, but I do not remember my father receiving pressure over the loss. The decision to keep the Fair open a second year was a popular one.

My parents attended many official functions hosted by the participating countries, but their main pleasure was to walk the Fair. They were not well-traveled and so enjoyed being exposed to other countries; they particularly liked the Japanese Pavilion and the Chinese Village.

I was in college at the time and worked during the summer as a guide. There was no criticism of my getting a job with my father on the Board of Directors. That's how things were done in those days.

The guides and guards all fell under the same category — serving the public. We were in uniform,

> *The administration did not have to go out and sell the community on the Exposition. There were few, if any, opposition groups.*

blue coats and yellow pants. We also wore police badges. The guides were used primarily for special events. We were to keep order, answer questions, and direct guests who were lost. The guards were assigned to stations, and we were to move around continually in that station, be it a concert area, a building or several buildings. We were supposed to be visible and, of course, observant. I don't remember what the pay was, but it was good by college students' standards. It was such a good job that I stayed out of college the fall semester to continue working there. My answer to my parents' objections was that I would make enough money working to pay for the rest of my college education, which I did.

All the companies with exhibits, IBM, the telephone company, and so forth, hired local people just as trade shows do now. There was a lot of interaction between employees. From the social standpoint it was a lot of fun. The girls hired were mostly local girls who had just graduated from high school, and many dates were planned when we all got off work. There was a lot to do — restaurants, exhibits, concerts, shows, dances, even at one time a circus. It was a college student's paradise.

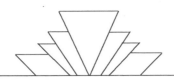

VIVIAN GIROD

When the City Fathers were talking about having an exposition, they asked, "Who shall we have do the flowers?" Mr. Herbert Fleishacker was President of the Park Commission at that time, and he said, "I know just the one. Julius Girod. You won't be sorry." So they took his word for it and decided to use my husband.

Julius was born out by the Cliff House in San Francisco. His father was in charge of Sutro Gardens there. Julius had begun working at Golden Gate Park, picking up papers, when he was 14. Then when he finished high school, he went right on in the park system. John McLaren, of course, was Superintendent and he used to have special classes at night where he taught his gardeners. They learned a lot from him. Julius also studied landscaping at night. Before he died, he had worked 43 years there during which he held every single job.

He was Assistant Superintendent earning $800 a month when he was offered the position of Chief of the Bureau of Horticulture for the Fair. He took a leave of absence from the park, and for the same salary, accepted this new job. He and his staff spent one year in an office on Bush Street planning the whole thing. The next year the headquarters were moved to Balboa Park where they started the plantings.

Everything was planted according to when each flower would bloom. The bulbs, hundreds of thousands of bulbs, were put on ice so they wouldn't bloom too soon. That was quite a thing to figure out — to have everything blooming when the Fair opened. They used electricity, actually heating the soil, with some of the other plants. Each court was planned to highlight one particular color. For the blue court my husband wanted ceanothus. It grows wild, but it can be cultivated. It's a pretty thing, something like a thistle when it blooms. Everybody said, "It's too cold here to

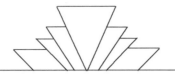

transplant ceanothus." My husband figured out that by heating the soil, he could do it. The soil and roots were heated in the main propagating house in Balboa Park and they did beautifully. The bamboo they got from Saratoga also needed that electricity while it was getting a good start.

Some of the men went all over the state to find trees and shrubs for the Fair. Everyone wanted to donate trees. The men would box them, bring them back on trucks, and take them over to the Island on barges. When the Fair opened, people wondered how they got such big trees to grow so fast.

Of course they had a soil problem. The Island did not exist until 1937 and the black soil that had been dredged up to make the Island was not good for planting. They had to leach it to get the salt out of it and then cover it with good top soil. But they figured that all out and the results were just beautiful.

My husband thought vegetables were as lovely as flowers, so he made one planting of ornamental chard — red cabbage. People had never before seen red cabbage used as a planting in a garden. Julius would lie awake at night thinking of all the things he was going to do. He got some of his most original ideas in the middle of the night.

Right by the entrance to the Fair was a large area that faced the wind and sea water and was a particularly difficult place for flowers to survive. Then in the middle of one night it came to Julius that mesmbryanthemum would be just right for the area. So they planted 25 acres of all colors of mesmbryanthemum. It was spectacular, and that one area was written up all over the country. Some called it "The Persian Rug," or "The Persian Prayer Rug," but Julius always called it "The Magic Carpet." Oh, he had such good ideas!

My favorite court was Lewis Hobart's. It was the pink court and had lovely rhododendrons. They do well in San Francisco, and they were at their best in that court. I just loved walking through the courts and the flowers. Of course I went to the exhibits while I was there, but the flowers were the main thing for me.

My husband made many friends at the Fair. The

The bulbs, hundreds of thousands of bulbs, were put on ice so they wouldn't bloom too soon.

Emperor of Japan sent his own gardener to do the gardens around the Japanese exhibits, and I remember a big reception for this gardener, quite a to-do. He and my husband became good friends and enjoyed working together. Art Linkletter was another of the friends we made at the Fair. He was an announcer there, and everyone liked him. He is a very intelligent, nice person. Marshall Dill, Leland Cutler, and Mayor Rossi were kind to my husband; in fact, through the years all the mayors were good to Julius.

For the second year of the Fair Elmer Gould took over Julius' job and Julius went back working under John McLaren. Many people don't realize that at the end of his life McLaren was blind, and my husband had to be his eyes, really. My husband's work was well known, particularly because of the Fair, and when John McLaren died, Julius was appointed Superintendent. Houses in San Francisco were in great demand then and the Commissioners said if we sold ours at 32nd and Lincoln Way we could live in McLaren Lodge in the Park. It was wonderful because the office was right there, too. We paid only $50 a month and that was for the utilities. It was like living in a mansion without the upkeep. Now, unfortunately, they have turned the whole thing into offices, ruining that wonderful home. But then it was the most beautiful place. I was really spoiled living there. It was the happiest time of our lives.

On Christmas, after we had been living in that home for six years, the *Examiner* called us in the middle of our family party, and said, "Do you know that you will have to leave by May 1st? You will have to give up that home and leave." The powers-that-be didn't let us know; the newspaper called us and told us. It ruined our Christmas. I had my whole family there, and our Christmas was ruined.

I have kept scrapbooks of the Fair, mainly my husband's part in it, but my prize is the picture I keep in my bedroom. Julius used to have it in his office, an oil painting over a photograph of the rhododendron gardens at the Hobart Court.

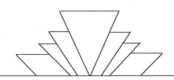

ALICE ZEISZ

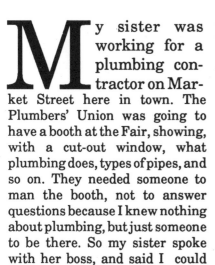

My sister was working for a plumbing contractor on Market Street here in town. The Plumbers' Union was going to have a booth at the Fair, showing, with a cut-out window, what plumbing does, types of pipes, and so on. They needed someone to man the booth, not to answer questions because I knew nothing about plumbing, but just someone to be there. So my sister spoke with her boss, and said I could stop at Treasure Island on my way back from UC and stay there in the afternoons and evenings. So that is how I got my job.

There was another young woman who worked with me, Ruth Coombs. I didn't know her well. People would ask questions and we had literature to pass out. When people walked by we would get them into conversations. It was interesting and fun. You met so many people from out of town, and people from the other booths would come over and talk.

I have a picture of the National Women's Party booth, which was in the same building where I worked.

Alice Zeisz stood behind the Plumbers' Union display at the Fair. She now spends part of her time in Sonoma where her family grows grapes.

It was managed by Jean Meece, and my friend Catherine Kenny worked there. On the wall of the exhibit were pictures of Elizabeth Cady Stanton and Susan B. Anthony, and a large sign: "Men and Women Shall Have Equal Rights Throughout the United States and Every Place Subject to its Jurisdiction." Imagine, in 1939!

The Mormons had a big exhibit in the center of the building. The young Mormon men often went home on the same ferry boat as we did. One night my friend decided to take the Mormons on. She went over to them and said, "You know, I really don't know why you think your religion is so good." Well, away they went! Later I said to her, "Why did you do that?" They were very nice gentlemen, but their big thing was converting people.

Most of the people who worked at the Fair were my age. Some of the young fellows who went to Santa

117

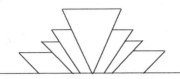

A L I C E Z E I S Z

Clara worked in the summer as guards. They stayed in boarding houses on Pacific Avenue and worked at the Fair for some extra money. We would go with them to the dances in the evenings.

I was asked to try out for the Aquacade. I loved swimming, but I was too shy to do such a thing. But I did meet several of the girls they recruited for that. I remember double dating with some of them.

I was lucky because I had graduated from high school, and when my parents asked what I would like

> *I was asked to try out for the Aquacade. I loved swimming, but I was too shy to do such a thing.*

for a present I said I would like to go to the New York Fair. My father was a railroad man, so I had a railroad pass. That made it possible for me to go. Seeing that Fair was entirely different from working at ours. The New York Fair was more elaborate. But I don't think the flowers were as nice, nor the lighting at night.

I felt very lucky to work at the San Francisco Fair. When my sister was setting it up for me I thought, "Oh, that is just the nicest thing that could happen to me." And it was.

Opposite: The graceful statue of the Evening Star, designed by Ettore Cadorin, stands over the Court of the Moon. The coquettish figure holds a star in her hand.

118

Above: For most San Franciscans, the Folies Bergère was their first taste of sophisticated French entertainment. The box office admitted lots of "college students" whose voices hadn't yet changed. Opposite top: President Marshall Dill enlivened the Fair's musical offerings the second year by booking such big-name talents as Benny Goodman and his band. They drew throngs of people who found it difficult to sit still while listening to the clarinetist and his swinging band.

122

Opposite top: The National Cash Register Company tallied each day's attendance on an enormous counter. Paul Mantz and other stunt fliers often streaked the sky with smoke trails before swooping under the bridge.
Opposite bottom: The Redwood Empire Building, funded by Northern California counties, was faced with redwood bark and resembled a giant stump.
Above: The highly imaginative Gayway concession, "World of a Million Years Ago," gave visitors a taste of prehistoric life.

Opposite top and above: The Cavalcade of the Golden West (1939) and the Cavalcade of America (1940) took place on the world's largest stage and featured re-enactments of Custer's last stand, the completion of the transcontinental railroad, and the discovery of America. Herb Caen once played the role of General Custer with Jerry Bundsen as his Indian assistant. According to the official guide book, "A colored water-screen, 40-feet high, replaces a curtain across the 400-foot stage. Scenic effects are mounted on wheeled platforms operated on rails."
Opposite bottom: A well-dressed audience, including one woman wearing a fashionable snood, watches Ralph Murray's Exposition Band featuring Victor Kress on trumpet, and a line-up of beautiful girls.
(Photo by Charles C. Friel, courtesy Marjanne Pearson)

Overleaf: A real train steams onto the stage of the Cavalcade of the Golden West in a pageant re-enacting the hammering of the golden spike in Promontory, Utah, marking the completion of the transcontinental railroad.

In 1940 Billy Rose's Aquacade was brought in to improve attendance at the Fair. Starring Esther Williams, Gertrude Ederle, and Johnny Weissmuller, the Aquacade gave employment to dozens of Bay Area swimmers. It was the first exhibition of synchronized swimming most San Franciscans had ever seen, and was wildly popular.

*One of the Fair's main attractions for children was Salici's Puppet
Show; four generations of the Salici family kept tykes spellbound with
puppets and dancing marionettes, in a tradition which began in Italy
more than 400 years ago.*

Above: The severe vertical lines of the Federal Building are flanked by two brilliant murals: "Conquering of the West by Water" and "Conquering of the West by Land." The 48 104-foot columns represented the 48 states. Inside, at a cost of $1.5 million, the Pageant of America offered seven acres of exhibits showing "the story of the creation of a new civilization in a new world." (Courtesy Treasure Island Museum)

Left: The sawtooth portal in the Court of Reflections affords a view of the Arch of the Winds. (Courtesy Treasure Island Museum)

Opposite top: In the Court of Pacifica, the 80-foot Pacifica theme statue of the Exposition dwarfs visitors below.

Opposite bottom: A metal prayer curtain, 48-feet wide by 100-feet high, changed colors behind the statue throughout the evening.

Above: The Fair, as seen from Yerba Buena Island, glows in the twilight on a calm evening. (Courtesy Treasure Island Museum)
Left: The Tower of the Sun lives up to its name just before sunset. (Courtesy Treasure Island Museum)

Above: At night the view from Yerba Buena shows the fabulous jeweled city that so many Fair-goers remember. (Courtesy Treasure Island Museum)
Right: The Tower of the Sun, flanked by tall cloth banners, resembles a glowing rocket ship. (Courtesy Treasure Island Museum)

*Above: Blue spotlights form a fan
behind the statue of the
Evening Star.
Left: The Tower of the Sun is
mirrored in the Siesta Pools of the
Court of Reflections, designed
by L.P. Hobart.
Many of the 211,000 people who
attended the last day, September 29,
1940, remember the exact moment
when the lights went out for the last
time. That moment seemed not only
the end of the Fair and a decade, but
also the end of the peaceful world
they knew.*

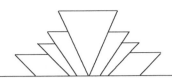

JOE SPRINZ

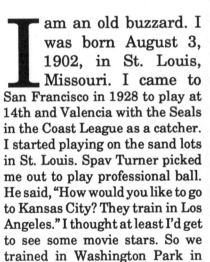

I am an old buzzard. I was born August 3, 1902, in St. Louis, Missouri. I came to San Francisco in 1928 to play at 14th and Valencia with the Seals in the Coast League as a catcher. I started playing on the sand lots in St. Louis. Spav Turner picked me out to play professional ball. He said, "How would you like to go to Kansas City? They train in Los Angeles." I thought at least I'd get to see some movie stars. So we trained in Washington Park in Los Angeles, and when we came back I was called in by the general manager who said, "Joe, I have no room for an extra catcher. We could send you home or we could try to get you a job somewhere else."

So I went off to my room, and I said a few prayers to make the right decision. You see, my parents didn't have a phone. The next morning I didn't want to go back to St. Louis and have people say I was chicken, so I said I would take a crack at it. They sent me to Enid, Oklahoma.

The first team for which I played professionally was Enid. $150 a month. We learned how to cook, sew,

Joe Sprinz, a well-known catcher for the San Francisco Seals, gained greater fame when, at the Fair, he caught a baseball, dropped from a blimp, square on his jaw.

wash our own clothes, and press our pants. We used to put them underneath the mattress and sleep on them all night. That's the way we pressed them. It was rough. That was professional ball in 1924. The next year I went to Shawnee, Oklahoma, because their catcher got hurt and the teams liked to help one another out.

Later I was traded to Arkansas City. A first baseman, a third baseman, and myself were traded to Arkansas City for a third baseman. I said, "We ought to quit. They don't think much of us. They traded three of us for one guy." The guy was hitting 400 and everyone thought he was pretty good until one of the catchers on the other team picked up his bat and saw that he had flattened it. After he was found out, he hit under 300.

I was with Arkansas City until I was sold to Des Moines where we won the pennant in 1926. In 1928 I

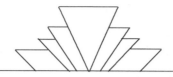

was sold to the San Francisco Seals for $15,000.

That was when I met my wife, Winifred. She came from Yugoslavia but had been raised in St. Louis. She was a baseball fan and when she heard I was from St. Louis, she wrote to me. She and her sister invited me to their apartment for dinner. I was attracted to Winifred. She was a nice looking woman, and it was a terrific dinner. You know, when you are on the road, you don't get home cooking. You eat in restaurants, so I enjoyed myself at her home.

But that winter I was sold to Indianapolis, and then later went to Cleveland. Then I couldn't get together with the business manager about salary, and they suspended me. I went home for about a month, then Branch Rickey, general manager for the St. Louis Cardinals, sent me a letter to come to see him. When I went into his office he was shuffling papers. I said, "What have you in mind, Branch?" Everybody called him Mr. Rickey. But he said, "Will you go down to Houston?" And I said, "It depends on how they are going to pay me." And he said, "Well, pretty good."

We won the pennant that year. The next year I went with the St. Louis Cardinals and I had the pleasure of rooming with Dizzy Dean. He and Pepper Martin and I used to go out and drink a couple of beers together. Dizzy Dean wasn't as screwy as they say he was. He had confidence; he'd pop off, but he could produce.

Winifred and I were corresponding all this time, including later when I went to Baltimore and back to Indianapolis. Finally, when I got back to San Francisco in 1937 to play with the Missions, she and I got married. When the Missions moved to Hollywood, I had the chance to stay in San Francisco with the Seals. So that turned out pretty good. I stayed with them for the rest of my baseball career.

Winifred and I had just one boy, Leroy. Perhaps we should have married earlier. I didn't know what to do. See, my father was out of work. The brewery shut down during Prohibition for a year and a half, and beside my parents, there were two sisters without any income. So if I had gotten married and had children, I would have had two families. I used to send money

Before I could get my glove on to catch it — pow, I got hit in the mouth.

back home. My sister used to say the Mother was always waiting for my check.

Baseball was 100 years old in 1939 and Walter Mails, a great left-handed pitcher, thought of an idea for a publicity stunt for the Seals. Mails got Woodall, Leonard and myself to go out on Treasure Island, and Lefty O'Doul went up to the top of the Tower of the Sun, 450 feet, and dropped balls for us to catch. I caught five, Woodall caught three, and Leonard, the other catcher, caught one or two, and gave up. One of the balls bounced off the concrete and came up about 20 feet. I told Woodall that if it had hit us, it would have killed us.

Well, Mails wasn't satisfied with that. He got the idea to get a dirigible to fly over Treasure Island and drop the balls down. They had a baseball field at the Fair, so about a week later we went out on that field, all in our uniforms. One by one they started to drop off, and soon I was the last one on the field. When I was a kid in St. Louis, we used to play "Cock-a-leader." Like, if you didn't dive into the Mississippi River to swim, or jump across a hole where they were digging, you were chicken. So I said to myself, "God hates a coward. I guess I'm it."

The dirigible came by and the pilot dropped one ball and it went into the stands. Then the next ball came and it dropped into the ground. I picked it up and thought, "Boy, that was buried pretty good." So the third one came down, and I saw that one all the way. You see, in those days, with a clear sky, you always put your hand up to shade your eye so that you could see the ball. Now they have glasses, but I didn't have anything then, just the catcher's glove.

Now, nobody told me the danger — how fast it would be coming down. Nobody told me the velocity doubles every 16 feet. If you're throwing a ball you might be throwing 100 miles an hour. The catcher sees it before it's on top of him. Well, here I saw this ball, but it looked like an aspirin, it looked so small. Before I could get my glove on to catch it — pow, I got hit in the mouth.

My neck was the worst thing. It felt like it was broken. The ball lacerated my lips. Still have the scars, and it busted a couple of teeth. On the way to the

136

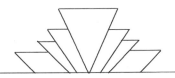
hospital in the ambulance I talked to myself. "Stay with 'em, Joe. Stay with 'em."

I had heard if you ever got badly hurt and passed out you might not make it. I got that idea from Cliff Brady, a guy I had known in St. Louis. Cliff told me once that he knew someone who got caught in an elevator that had kind of crushed his stomach. After they stopped the elevator, saved the kid and got him in the ambulance, Cliff said the kid talked all the time until they arrived at the hospital. The doctor there said if he had stopped talking and had gone to sleep, he probably would never have made it. So that's why all the time I was in the ambulance I kept saying, "Stay with 'em, Joe."

They took me to St. Joseph's Hospital, and I was there for about three months. While I was there I got acquainted with one of the nuns. I think her name was Sister Lorenzia, a one-armed German nun. She took good care of me. Ted Norbett used to get boxes of Wheaties whenever he hit a home run, and he didn't know what to do with them all. I asked him if we could give the Wheaties to the nuns. They were glad to get them.

The first time I went before a pitcher again, it didn't bother me. God was good to me. He gave me the guts to go out there and play ball without being shaky or anything like that. I was fortunate to still continue to play ball and not to lose my nerve. I had headaches

> *On the way to the hospital in the ambulance I talked to myself. "Stay with 'em Joe. Stay with 'em."*

for about five years, but they finally went away. I guess all the stuff and parts God made me out of had to get back together again. It jogged up my apple butter, but I didn't get ball shy.

During my first year in baseball I was in a slump once, and one of the old-timers, Joe Rempe, said to me, "Joe, do you want to go out?" So we went out and had a few beers that night and when we were playing the next day that sun was beating on my head and I had to bear down extra hard. I didn't want to get hit in the head because I already had a headache. After the accident, when I'd have a headache, I just tried extra hard.

I went to the Fair after that several times with my wife and son and other people I knew. It didn't bother me to be there. What the hell. Like one of the Jesuits, Father Duffy, told me, "Don't look back, Joe."

I enjoyed the Fair. It was entertaining. Like those swimmers at the Aquacade. They were beautiful, all those people swimming and working together. It was terrific. Just like playing baseball; just like a second baseman and shortstop. You work together.

Every once in a while I run into someone who says, "I was there when it happened." Even when my wife was dying and the neighbors and paramedics and the fire department were there, one of the firemen asked me if I was the one who tried to catch the ball from the blimp.

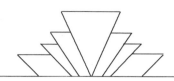

SERGE LAUPER

Y ou have to give credit to the officials of the Fair. They had great imagination, determination, and courage to attempt a thing like that right after the Depression. They built an island and made such a beautiful place of it. They showed the world what San Francisco could do.

I thought it was pretty clever of them to invite everyone to be a part of the Fair. Whether it was a school, a band, a state, an opera star, or a business, they were all invited to participate.

I remember we had two or three different days called Utah Day. There was a chamber of commerce approach to those days, to tell everyone the advantages of Utah, to promote the mines, the farming, the enterprises and the natural beauty of the state.

One of the exhibits was that of the Latter Day Saints. We are a missionary church, and we have a great interest in telling people about the church and then letting them decide for themselves. The missionaries who were assigned to this exhibit were the front-page type of young men, good speakers with pleasing presence. They offered tracts and books on the Church and answered questions about its beginnings and its intent.

There was a small replica of the Tabernacle of Salt Lake at the exhibit, maybe five feet by ten feet. That was the conversation piece. People had seen it on postcards, or some had heard the choir itself, on the oldest continuous radio program on the air, on Sunday mornings at 5:30 Pacific time. They knew about the building and its fine acoustics and were interested in the replica. Our exhibit was not a mecca for everyone, but those who came in were interested, and we got a lot of referrals.

My wife and I had three of our four children then, and we usually went to the Fair with the children. They were goggle-eyed, and always wanted us to stay longer. Sometimes we would take the last ferry out.

We really couldn't afford it, but we sampled some

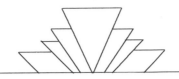

of the restaurants at the Fair, the ones that represented different cultures. What feeds one part of the world some people wouldn't even think of eating, and others would class as a delicacy. I remember the Indonesian and the Polynesian restaurants. I can still see the big roast pig they had in one of those places. Those restaurants were a forerunner of what we have now in San Francisco.

I have a microwave oven, and the first one I ever saw was there at the Fair.

I sometimes think of the marvels that I first saw on Treasure Island, things that are commonplace now. I have a microwave oven, and the first one I ever saw was there at the Fair. It was not the type you see on the market now, but it had the same principles. I saw them cook a potato in six or seven minutes. They said then that in a few years it would be commonplace, but I thought no, that's too much. That booth showed how light travels and how the voice can be picked up in short waves. Those demonstrations were marvelous.

You see, I'm 86 years old now. There have been a lot of changes in my lifetime. I remember the very first telephone that came to our area in Utah. It was one of those that hung on the wall that you would crank, and everybody along the line could listen in. When some neighbors got a phonograph, we traveled in our horse and buggy to their farm to see it. These neighbors decided to have an afternoon of socializing with the farmers in the community and they put on a demonstration of this marvelous thing which, with a cylinder, could make music. When the first crystal set radio came in 1921, I sat up all night listening to it. Now television slipped right through. It came along as a natural thing. Nobody paid any attention to it.

This Fair at Treasure Island was the first big fair I had ever seen. I had been to county fairs and farm fairs, and since then I have been to other world fairs. But they don't stand out in my mind like the one at Treasure Island. I never saw anything before or since that comes near the lighting they had there, the wonderful displays of light and water. I think of the whole island as fountains.

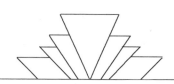

JEAN WOLF

I loved the Fair. At the time I was working in a lower Market Street office and it was easy enough after work to take the ferry to Treasure Island. The motion of the boat put me in a festive mood by the time we arrived at the slip on the Island.

I took the view of the city for granted and always looked to the Island both coming and going. As the ferry docked, there was a wind barrier in the mid-distance blocking the view of the Fair buildings. But in the foreground there was a gentle upward slope planted with ice plant. This was called the Magic Carpet. The ice plant blooms were magenta, hot pink, and other purples and reds and had a long blooming period. Beautiful vibrant colors like Bryce Canyon.

One of my friends at that time was a soldier who was stationed at the fairgrounds — good reason to visit the Fair frequently! His company was part of the daily flag ceremonies, and each member had earned this assignment through intense competition at his home base. They were good at what they did — showing off

Jean Wolf was a girl Friday in a credit union office on Market Street. After her marriage she became a full-time homemaker.

to the public their expert close order drill. I think they were also responsible for the fireworks which were set off close to their camp.

Originally I had come from central California and more recently Utah, and I was terribly impressed with urban sophistication. The General Motors exhibit of the clear plastic see-through hydromatic engine amazed me. To see this thing functioning, engaging and disengaging, was impressive. An early type of key punch card sorter was another bit of urban sophistication new to me. After an operator programmed the machine, all the little cards would be rapidly and automatically sorted in the designated slots. Amazing! The voice synthesizer, displayed by the telephone company, or Westinghouse, was operated by a person at a keyboard. The operator could electronically create voice tones and conduct conversations

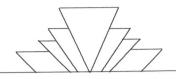

The Fair was more than just a theme park; it marked the end of a peaceful era.

with the spectators by playing the keyboard. Do you suppose that's who is answering our directory inquiries today?

What I truly enjoyed were the free Wednesday night symphonies. My sister, brother-in-law and I would sit in the arena listening to great music as we sipped homemade Cuba Libras from our Coke bottles. One night we were sitting in the side bleacher and we could see Jan Pierce, the soloist of the evening, take off his glasses just as he walked onto the stage. We watched as he almost walked straight ahead off the stage. Fortunately an orchestra member guided him into the turn just in time. Later I saw that he almost missed the death bed of Violetta in the last scene of "La Traviata."

I felt very privileged to be able to watch Diego Rivera and his assistants work on the huge mural in the Fine Arts Building. He was always in denim work clothes and spent much of the time directing the other painters. He was way up there on the scaffolding, but I knew who he was and was most impressed to be watching this larger-than-life man. In the biography of his wife, Frieda, there is an interesting account of this Treasure Island project.

In the same building were displays of affordably furnished rooms. The furniture was sold after the Fair closed, and my sister and her husband furnished their first apartment with some of it. The displays stressed the decorators' use of the new synthetics. The durability of these materials long outlasted their popularity in style.

There were two special places I went to every time I was on the Island. First was the promenade which displayed a statue of the Evening Star. The statue, a woman with a star, was commonly known as the chocolate girl because she resembled the woman on the Bakers Chocolate logo of the time. The other very pleasing and restful spot for me was the statue of St. Francis, situated in a circular planting of flowers. It was usually planted with Shasta daisies, impeccably kept. Remember, I had just come from Utah where we had snow all winter long, and to see an endless season of flowers and plantings at Treasure Island was impressive.

A pleasant snack area featured things Guatemalan — food, wine and the music of the Hurtado Brothers' Marimba Band. They were the best.

Seems to me the pleasing ambiance of the Fair came from the Bay site itself, the Art Deco aspect of the architecture, and the effective, not garish, use of colored lighting. The Fair was more than just a theme park; it marked the end of a peaceful era. Pretty much pre-plastic and pre-Disney. It was a haven between Depression and war and was indeed a magic time.

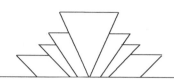

Fred, Inez, and Sister M. Estelle Small

Inez Small: We went to the Fair often, at least once a week, more often if we had visitors. I enjoyed all the exhibition halls so much. It was more than just an outing, like going to Golden Gate Park. The Fair was more exciting because we were going to see things we couldn't see every day.

My favorite statue was Pacifica, overlooking the Court of the Sun, and behind her was a curtain of stars. During the first year the stars had little bells which would tinkle in the breeze. Evidently some people objected, because during the second year the bells were removed.

Whenever we went I always drove. They had preferred parking for women, so we wouldn't have to walk so far. Seeing a woman driving, they'd let us park in the women's section, even though I had a man in the car.

Fred Small: We went to the fairs in Seattle and Spokane, but they weren't anything like this one. This Fair was much bigger, and had wonderful flowers. The admission couldn't have been too much, because I was

Fred and Inez Small visited the Fair with their two daughters. He worked as office manager for an import firm; she was a registered nurse. Sr. Estelle Small teaches at Mercy High School.

married and bringing up two children on a not-too-fabulous salary. But we never went to the Folies or expensive things like that. We could spend a whole day on very little money.

The children enjoyed the Gayway and all the funny things. The Headless Woman sat with her legs crossed looking perfectly normal except that she had no head. We wanted to get some itching powder and put it on her legs. Our children used to play Headless Woman when they got home. The second year they had Ripley's Believe It Or Not, and he exposed the whole thing, showed how they did it with mirrors.

The Cavalcade of America was spectacular. They had a long, outdoor stage, and they brought on horses and engines with the trains, re-enacting the hammering of the spike at Utah. I don't think they used a real gold spike.

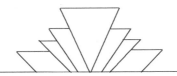

The first time I saw television was at the Fair. There were two rooms; you looked at the television picture in one room and someone with you would go into another room and you could see him on a black and white screen of about 17 inches.

At the phone company display people would line up to make free phone calls to anywhere in the United States. On the wall was a large map, and when your phone call went through a light on the map would shine to indicate where you were calling.

One place served English scones and jam; we used to go there for supper. Then we'd stay on for the evening lights.

Sister M. Estelle Small: My sister and I were very small — we must have been six and nine — but I can remember going to the Fair quite frequently. I can remember, too, that we used to try to get any kind of handout. Anything. My father made a wooden chest for us, just for all the literature we got from the Fair. In fact, it's still upstairs. He painted it and put a decal on it of a little girl dancing. My sister and I divided all the brochures and souvenirs.

One thing which we always used to try to get were the silver coins. They must have been aluminum because they were very light; Union Pacific Railroad gave them away. The petroleum exhibit gave ones with a gold finish. We'd get as many of those as we could. It was like getting money. The Heinz exhibit used to give out little pickle pins that were about three-quarters of an inch long and said Heinz on them, so we would wear our pickles home. We just went around like pack rats acquiring as much as we could get our

I can remember, too, that we used to try to get any kind of handout. Anything.

hands on.

The Pennsylvania Railroad gave out tinted 3-D glasses to use when we watched their movie. It was on a small screen and I remember a train coming right at us. There were many things that were just beginning then, like the 3-D movie and television. All these innovations were just about ready for birth. After the war they were developed, but at this time they were just on the horizon.

An electronic voice called the Vodor was on a stage. It didn't move. It was like a decoration on the wall, but the speech mechanism was behind the face so you thought the voice came from the face. It would actually talk to people, but it also had its own slogan which it frequently repeated: "Patience is necessary, and so is expe-e-e-erience."

I liked the Japanese Exhibit. I liked the color, the women in the kimonos. You could watch silkworms making silk. It was all so different from our culture.

This Fair wasn't just another Disneyland. There was entertainment, yes, but there was more to it. Little kids don't say to themselves, "How much am I learning?" We just liked going for the day, but we really were learning things. I was too young then to think about going to the countries whose exhibits were at the Fair. First of all, we didn't have the money, and people then just didn't do that kind of traveling. I have since gotten the bug.

There were always many people there, but it was never too crowded. There was a tradition about our trips to the Fair. We always went back to the Vodor and to the headless girl, and we always had scones. We would see other things, too, but we had those favorites.

143

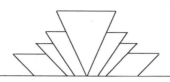

VICTOR AND FLORENCE KRESS

Victor Kress: My father didn't have the chance to go to high school. He had to work to help support his family. He had medals from grammar school and the principal begged his parents to let him go on to high school, but it didn't do any good. Yet he became a college professor.

As a young boy he played music on the side with groups such as the Columbia Park Boys Club. That club had all kinds of activities. Once they hiked from San Francisco to Eureka and back.

My father was working for Southern Pacific when World War I broke out. His friends joined the Navy band, and they needed my dad in the band. So he quit his job, didn't tell his mother, and got on the battleship *Oregon*. He was sworn into the Navy as they sailed through the Golden Gate. It was on that ship that he met Ralph Murray, who played tuba in the Navy band.

After the war Ralph Murray conducted the Golden Gate Park Band, and my father played trumpet for him for more than forty years. He played in the

Victor Kress's father played the trumpet in Ralph Murray's Band at the Fair and taught music. Both Victor and Florence visited the Fair as children.

San Francisco Symphony over forty years as well. Later my father earned a prestigious reputation as a music teacher privately, at the San Francisco Conservatory and San Francisco State. Two years after he retired from State the whole band came over and played for an hour in front of his house on Sloat Boulevard and presented him with a plaque in appreciation.

My mother was the business person. She planned the finances and investments. She was always giving my father the devil for giving free lessons to people who couldn't afford them.

During the summers of 1939 and 1940, my father, as trumpet player in Ralph Murray's Exposition Band, played at the Fair every day. The musicians had a lot of fun together. Once some of them nailed my father's shoes to the floor. He went to pick up his change of shoes and everyone laughed.

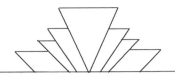

He would take me over to the Fair with him, and I usually wandered about the fairgrounds by myself. At first workers there thought I was lost, but I never was. I was nine. Sometimes my cousin came with me. Once we got hold of some gunpowder from the Cavalcade and lit it off.

I seldom went to the Gayway. It chewed up the money, and there were so many free places to go. I'll always remember the big vats of chocolate, and the Heinz exhibit with the bins of pickles. There was a mining exhibit where you could actually go down into the mine. One exhibit featured test tubes and bottles where they showed fetuses at different stages, and various animals, such as bats, preserved in formaldehyde. I liked going into the model home. Later it was moved to 26th and Crestlake, where it still sits. I think it was the first split-level house in San Francisco. I remember the Folies Bergère was a show with elaborate costumes. I often went to see the marionettes. I admired the carving on the figures. The fellow who ran the show taught me some of the tricks, and I started carving puppets myself.

> *Once some of them nailed my father's shoes to the floor. He went to pick up his change of shoes and everyone laughed.*

It was an interesting era. At the Fair and in San Francisco people were friendly; you'd ride a streetcar and someone would say "Hello, how are you?" and you'd talk to them. But as soon as the war was over that all dropped away.

Florence Kress: I remember being at the Fair and walking into a movie showing a woman having twins. My sister and I wandered into it. I was seven; she was five. I don't know how Mom knew we were there, but suddenly we were yanked out. I'll never forget that.

The chocolate vats were huge, with big beaters going around. That memory remains with me because I was a chocolate freak even then.

My sister Katie and I had our picture taken with a midget. That felt weird because I was young, and this woman was much shorter than I was.

My mother belonged to the Women's City Club. They had a little building of their own there. After we walked around we could go in and relax.

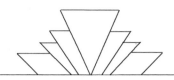

HERB CUNNINGHAM

I was a young boy, 11 years old when the Fair opened, and we lived in Santa Cruz. My dad was a concessionaire at the beach there. He applied to run a photo booth at the '39 Exposition, and he started working at Treasure Island about six months before the Fair opened, taking the pass photos. My father had a little office in the Administration Building and had to walk about 12 feet into the woman's rest room in order to get to his office. The women would say, "You don't want to come in here," and he would say, "Oh yes, I do."

As well as taking the pictures for the passes he had four photo concessions once the Fair opened. The customer would walk in and be seated at the right height. The lady working there would say, "Look here," press a button, and take four pictures. She would then run them through four chemicals. When that was done she would either carry them out or push them through a slot, and the customer would take them. My father could afford to have somebody there because once the pictures came out the employee would try to sell an enlargement. She would take the best picture and say, "Why don't you get an enlargement of this one?" If a movie star ever happened to walk by, he or she would practically be dragged in to have a picture taken. That picture would then be put up so that people passing by would be sure to see it.

The pictures had to be rinsed in water, but there was no water in the booths. My father or one of his employees had to carry water to them.

My father always said people like to have their picture taken. They'd put the pictures in their cigar boxes and never see them again. But there is something about getting your picture taken.

Although my mother usually stayed in Santa Cruz to take care of business there, she sometimes worked at the Fair in one of the photo booths next to a handwriting analysis place. She listened and figured

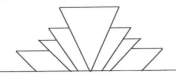

out that most of the predictions were just general. "You'll meet a new friend within three weeks" — that kind of thing. One day the woman there said, "Can you take over for me for a few minutes?" My mother was agreeable, so she took over for 20 minutes. After that, every time that woman wanted a break, my mother analyzed handwriting. There is some science to handwriting analysis, but there was no science to it at the Fair.

During those years, my father had an apartment in San Francisco. When I came up to visit the Fair, I stayed with him. But since he'd be working, I'd have most of the time to wander around the Fairgrounds by myself. The exhibit I remember the most was the Chinese Village. They had acrobats jumping through hoops and doing pyramids. Boy, they were really good!

The first time I saw television was at the San Francisco Fair. I remember distinctly the tube was down in the set. You looked at the image in a mirror. They hadn't figured out how to reverse the images electronically, I guess.

There was a place in the industrial exhibit where they had a Greyhound bus which was the first of what they called the Silver Sides. It was, of course, a very comfortable bus. The idea was to walk through this bus, but when I was tired I would sit down for 15 or 20 minutes. It was the most comfortable place to rest on the Island.

> *The women would say, "You don't want to come in here," and he would say, "Oh yes, I do."*

There was nothing like the grandeur of the Cavalcade, the horses galloping, the steam trains, everybody singing and dancing. They do that in the movies, but that was right out there on the stage.

At the entrance to the Gayway was a guy who sold two little pieces of aluminum put together, and he called them "Hum-a-tunes." You would put them in your mouth and hum. Remember putting wax paper around a comb and putting it in your mouth and humming? Well, it was the same idea. He would demonstrate this thing, and he was really clever at it. He would get a crowd there and he would say, "Anybody can play this." To prove his point, he would give one to a little kid in the crowd to try. The first time he gave me one I could do it pretty well. After that I'd go by about four or five times a day. He'd see me coming, and I would work my way down front. He would give me one, and I'd play it. I got to be pretty good at it. I never talked to him, but I was a shill for him the whole time I was up there.

One interesting thing — when you went to the parking lot, you would see Japanese out there with their cameras taking pictures one right after another. Almost every day you would see this. They must have had pictures of the whole Bay, Treasure Island, and everything around. It was only later that my folks remembered that and connected it with the War.

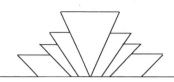

SISTER KAREN MARIE

The Fair was about the biggest thing to happen to us when we were children. We went almost every day. The second year my mother bought season tickets for my sister and me, and in that year we went one hundred and one times. I have never met anyone else who went so often but maybe someone did.

I remember going over with my mother, my sister, my friend, and my friend's mother, and our mothers would let us loose for the day. I guess that was our first experience of freedom. Then at night we would meet our mothers and go home. Most often we got to stay until the Fair ended and we would hear our good friend Paul Bohegian sing "When You Come To the End of a Perfect Day" as the outdoor show closed. The Fair ended each night of the second year with fireworks, which we watched all the way home.

I remember the Gayway and "Have you seen Stella?" I used to imitate that barker who graveled out that come-on. I remember the midgets and the man who bonged out your weight and if he did not guess it,

Sister Karen Marie went to the Fair almost every day when she was 11 and 12. She entered the Dominican Order and has been an educator in the Bay Area for many years.

you'd get a doll. I always looked lighter than I was, so I would win every time. We would spend hours at the Coca Cola exhibit watching the bottles fill up. We visited the Norwegian Ski Lodge and other houses that were models, and we went almost daily to the Chinese Village. We were crazy about George Jue, the manager, who was especially nice to us. We watched Ralph Murray's Band and especially one of the band members, Victor Kress. I remember the colorful lights behind the Statue of Pacifica. They were magical. I recall the organ grinders and "Beer Barrel Polka," the Elephant Trains, and the big Cash Register that told how many people were at the Fair. The U.C. science exhibit displayed embryos in bottles and wax models with goiters. I was thrilled with the Java exhibit of real shrunken heads. I felt sorry for my school friends whose parents did not take them to the Fair.

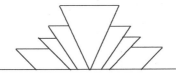

The Pacific Telephone and Telegraph Company had one electronic device which enabled you to hear your own voice, and another where you could test your hearing, but the main display looked like a bingo game set-up. You were given a number and you waited for a chance to win a free telephone call to anywhere in the United States. A numbered ping pong ball was periodically chosen from a cage, and if you had the lucky number you could make a free telephone call to anywhere in the United States. If you waited there any length of time at all, you could win one of these. I had a pen pal in Appleton, Wisconsin, so it was great fun to telephone her. The only drawback was that all around the counter were telephones and stools and everyone passing by could pick up a phone and listen in to your conversation, a demonstration of the marvel of long-distance telephoning.

I remember a machine where you could test your driving ability. Although I knew nothing about driving a car, I was quite proud that my score indicated I was skilled at it.

But most of all I remember the great shows at the Fair. Senor Wences was the best ventriloquist we had ever seen. Ted Lewis always started his show with "Is everybody HAPPY?" Tommy Dorsey, Phil Harris, all the big bands. The Folies Bergère — some people thought it was terrible that we children were allowed to go to the Folies, but we loved them and went time after time. That was a treat because it was expensive.

But the best show of all was the one sponsored by the American Society of Composers, Authors, and Publishers; I'll never forget it. You couldn't believe all the wonderful people on that show. One of the highlights was Harry Armstrong who sang "Sweet Adeline." Jerome Kern played "All the Things You Are," while Tony Martin sang. The composers who played and sang their own songs were so talented and spirited that Judy Garland, who was also on the program and sang "Somewhere over the Rainbow" was not particularly good by comparison. That show was so great that lines formed for hours before so people could get in. The friend who always went with us started singing and pretty soon the whole crowd just sang and sang as we waited to get into the show.

The ride over and back on the Ferry was always

> *I was thrilled with the Java exhibit of real shrunken heads.*

fun. My mother, who could not tell one movie star from another, could spot writers a mile away. One day she said, "That's Theodore Dreiser." Of course we did not know who Theodore Dreiser was, but my sister asked for his autograph. He was gruff and said he did not give autographs, but his wife was very nice and a few minutes later, while we were still on the ferry, she came over and gave us her husband's autograph. I remember Paul Gallico, too. He was giving a talk at the Fair, and he answered a question about whether he minded if his audiences got bored during his talks. He said that he didn't usually mind, but that it did bother him whenever anyone would start shaking his watch.

Before the Fair San Francisco was such an exciting place. The parade down Market Street to celebrate the bridges was so wonderful that no parades since have seemed very good to me. Everyone got ready for the Fair. Just before it opened the whole city celebrated with an enthusiasm we have never duplicated. The district stores, as well as the big downtown ones, had false fronts, making the whole city look like a mining town. Everyone had something western or Spanish to wear for the fiesta. I can still remember the wonderful smell of a leather holder through which I looped a colorful cowboy bandana. I wore that with a black Spanish hat with yellow pompoms around the rim. I guess I wanted to be both Spanish and a cowgirl. One day my father arrived home late from work. He had been in the hoosegow. He had grown neither beard nor a mustache for the celebration so he was plucked from the street and put into a cage-like jail cell right out in the open. Although he was guilty of being clean shaven, he did have the fiesta spirit and enjoyed the whole experience.

My sister and I took dancing lessons. We were part of the O'Neill Sisters Kiddie Reviews that performed at the Golden Gate Theater. In 1938 we did a dance in denim pants and workshirts and used scrub brushes to clean the stage floor while we sang "We're Going to Shine for '39." Our pictures were in the papers a couple of times wearing pirate costumes to advertise the Fair. Then, later, we and our friends were lucky enough to dance at the Fair, too. Those were upbeat days in San Francisco, a special time.

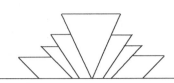

PHYLLIS BERNERO

T he first thing you saw when you came to the Fair was the Magic Carpet. I don't know how long it was, but it was as far as your eye could see, this incredible ice plant in every color of the rainbow. It was breathtaking. It knocked your socks off. And the first thing you heard was the carillon coming from the Tower of the Sun.

I was eleven in 1939. I almost always went to the Fair with two girls I met when I started kindergarten, their mother, and mine. We all had admission books. It's hard to believe the little book that we had with a ticket for every day's admission cost only one dollar. It was a little red book with pink tickets and we were threatened with our lives not to lose it. We had to carry the books ourselves because our pictures were on them and the gatekeepers would look to see if they matched.

My mother wrote a column for *The Sunset News*, a district paper at that time. She would write timely articles about the Fair. We knew pretty much what we were going to see each day, and the timing, because the activities would always be listed in the *Chronicle*. Usually our parents let us go once we got on the Island and we would meet them at the clock tower outside the Coca Cola building at a certain time.

The Fair had a special place in the Fine Arts Palace where they showed silent movies. The one I remember most of all, because we caused a disturbance by being a little cracked up by Lillian Gish's drama, was "Broken Blossoms." We were giggling and here were some of these older people who had been there for the silent movies and they were crying. We had to leave because we couldn't stop laughing.

One of our favorite treats was to go to the White Star Tuna building, which was round with a round counter in the middle. It was there I first had frozen peas. They were a big thing at that time. The waitresses would give you a flaky, stuffed-full-of-tuna turnover and cover it with a marvelous sauce and

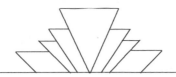

serve it with a portion of green peas. To us it was the epitome of haute cuisine.

Shows went on constantly at the Fair. There were high-wire acts out in the open. The trapeze artists worked without a net, up there in the fog. One man would go up a pole, stand on his head, and swing back and forth in the wind and fog. It scared me to death.

Jo-Jo the Clown conducted a children's amateur hour every day. I remember getting up there and doing an imitation of President Roosevelt, a silly little thing. "My dear friends, We are having more dam trouble, Boulder Dam, Coulee Dam, and all the dams are leaking." Children in those days didn't use words like "damn."

The ASCAP show was held toward the back end of the Island, not far from where they had the fireworks at night. When we heard they were going to have that show we leapt on it right away. The show was to be one night only, and we knew that would be one thing that would draw thousands of people. Our parents decided we had better stake it out early in the afternoon. We were among the first in line. Pretty soon other people started gathering. It was first come, first serve, a free performance. The crowd kept getting bigger, and bigger, and bigger. So I decided we should keep busy.

I got up and started leading people in song. I think my friends were embarrassed at first, but pretty soon it caught on. We were right in front, and I stood up on a bench so people could see me. I sang, leading them, for a couple of hours. My parents used to sing at home a lot, and when we would be in the car they would sing, so I knew a lot of songs from the '20s. So besides the songs we learned at school, like "My Country 'Tis of Thee" and "Poppies, Golden Poppies," I had them singing the oldies. Someone in the crowd passed a note up to my mother saying he was a talent scout. We never

> *I remember getting up there and doing an imitation of President Roosevelt, a silly little thing.*

did anything about that, but it is fun to think of what might have been.

I shall never forget the program itself once we finally got in and it started. All the composers of the time were there — George M. Cohan, Carrie Jacobs Bond, Joe Howard, Hoagy Carmichael, Irving Berlin, all of them.

I remember seeing Helen Keller at the Fair. She was there to give a lecture about her life. Her voice was a monotone. When I put together the fact that the woman was blind and deaf, it was phenomenal. After that sometimes I pretended to be blind and plugged my ears up and thought about her.

The Gayway was there for those who wanted that. The barkers were an art form, really. Even though many people went there, I don't think very many spent much time there. There was too much else to see.

One of the most fascinating things to watch was the sand painting done by Indians. They would smooth the sand, rake it so that it was without a ripple, and then take colored sand in their hands and make complicated designs, beautiful designs with the colored sand.

Airplanes were new then, and I really wanted to fly in one. For my 11th birthday, the first year of the Fair, my mother and my friends' parents went in to surprise me. They let the three of us take a ride in the seaplane. We had a tour over the Fair area and just a little bit of San Francisco. It was fantastic! I think the trip cost about $2.50, a bunch of money.

The fireworks! They were the most spectacular ones I've ever seen, and that's not just because of my age at the time. They had ducks that walked along, butterflies that moved their wings, and flags that waved.

The Fair was a very happy experience. The only negative thing I can think of is that it closed.

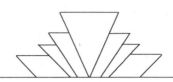

RICHARD REINHARDT

Richard Reinhardt visited the Fair often as a boy. The author of several books including Treasure Island: 1939-1940, he teaches journalism at UC Berkeley.

We watched the preparations for the Fair. As you would come and go on the ferries to cross the Bay you could see the bridges going up, and the island under construction. This island-building seemed such a wonderful thing. Another kid and I built an island in a creek in Oakland. It just seemed the thing that everyone should be doing.

The festivities and the build-up for the Exposition went on for several years. We were obsessed with it. I can't think of anything equivalent to it now. The Super Bowl or the World Series would be exciting and interesting to a lot of people, but not as absorbing to all ages and classes as the Fair was.

In a very uncritical way, the newspapers at that time would lend themselves to local things of that kind. I don't think any publication does that now. It was almost as if they had decided to become the PR vehicle for the Fair. You may have seen the headlines of the *Examiner* and *Chronicle* on the day the Fair opened, blazing headlines. They assigned reporters to the Fair months ahead of time, and then all during the Fair they had reporters who actually worked there in the Press Room on the Island interviewing celebrities who came and doing stories every day. They covered it as a beat just as they covered city government or the police.

I was tremendously excited about everything. In retrospect I think a lot of the Fair was shabby. The Gayway was really pretty shoddy. But the overall impression, the flowers, the lighting at night, the scale of the buildings, the lagoons, the little boats, the flags waving in the breeze, all of these things seemed to me absolutely wonderful.

I was after adventure. My main effort was trying to get into the sex shows. I got into the Folies Bergère, which was really relatively tame; they didn't bat an eye when I announced that I was 17 years old, and I was, in fact, 12. I think the young women all wore

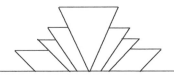

flesh-colored body stockings, so they were not as nude as they appeared to be. But I couldn't get into Sally Rand's Nude Ranch. I had a cousin from Kansas who was older than I, and he had an I.D. card that said he was a graduate student at KU. We thought the two of us could get in on this.

Like most kids then, I loved the free things, the frivolous things. There were free movies and free food samples. The Food Building was a wonderful place. You could have a little cup of Rancho Soup free, and you could get a little pin in a shape of a pickle that Heinz gave out. You could sample a Danish dessert called Junket made with rennet, a little like yogurt. It was considered very wholesome, a happy sort of dish. A lot of people were displaying gadgets, little machines with which you could make a radish into a rose or take all the peeling off an orange with one quick twist of your hand. These things were wonderful fun to look at.

I loved to go to the Federal Building which had exhibits of Indian life. Navajo Indians were dancing and doing sandpainting with colored sand. Also in that building were movies that had been produced by the WPA. One of them was about the dust bowl—the plowing practices and the erosion and drought that had caused that. Another was about the Mississippi River, a marvelous movie. And the puppet theater was delightful – all of these things going on at once.

People want to see things at world's fairs that they can't see anyplace else. That's part of the charm, to see something unique, to take an amusement ride which you can't take anywhere else, or to see a show that will never be performed in any other setting. The transitory quality of fairs causes us to remember them deeply, fondly. The fact that this Fair was going to vanish, and you knew it at the time, that this was only to last one summer, perhaps two, gave it a poignancy and an importance.

I can't say this Fair was unique. I don't think it had the kind of loving fan club, as it were, the strong nostalgia that the 1915 Exposition in San Francisco had. That seemed to have really gripped people's minds because of its beauty. Treasure Island was an

> *You could have a little cup of Rancho Soup free, and you could get a little pin in a shape of a pickle that Heinz gave out.*

attempt, in many ways, to recapture the beauty of 1915, although the architectural style was superficially different. If you look at it—if you examine it from a land-use perspective, let's say — it was really done on beaux-arts architectural principles, big courtyards with buildings symmetrical and harmonious around them, culminating in vistas. You would get these great vistas that you could take in with awe and delight.

In other words, it wasn't a "wander through" place at all. It wasn't the least bit like the Expo in Vancouver a year or so ago, where everything was connected by railroads and you moved around on a totally different principle. The 1939 Fair was laid out, in fact, by many of the same architects who had designed the 1915 Exposition. They were consciously seeking to bring back some of the feeling that that Fair gave, its grandeur and its harmony. They rejected the kind of architecture and urban design that was at the New York Fair. That Fair looked to the future, toward designing utopian cities. The famous perisphere and trylon were supposed to be perfect abstract architectural forms.

As somebody said, "New York looked to the future, and Treasure Island took a firm grasp on the past." That was, in itself, one of its best features, because that was what a lot of people in San Francisco wanted. They preferred to look back at 1915, certainly to jump over the '30s in their minds entirely, because San Francisco had been in a desperate situation in the 1930s.

I suppose that the very intervention of the war put a glow upon the memory of the 1939-40 Fair. Between 1939 and 1940 the war had broken out in Europe. The Germans had invaded Poland, but the war was in a somewhat quiescent state for close to a year. But Czechoslovakia had fallen to the Nazis and Austria had been annexed to Germany, and the threat of Hitler to Europe was very obvious. The war was very much on my mind, even at that age.

I would love to see another world's fair, but I'm not at all sure that the same type of fair is absolutely right. In the first place, if it had been on the mainland,

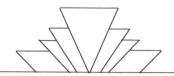

we would have gained some important civic buildings; instead, they are all gone. I think that was a great waste.

There is no particular reason that a fair has to be in one plot of ground any more than the Los Angeles Olympic Games were. The Olympic Games gained something by being spread over Southern California. There were great events in the Coliseum, equestrian events and races here and there, even soccer games in the Bay Area, at Stanford. I think that pattern makes a little more sense in an urban setting. If you have an Opera House, you might use that as part of the fair. The fair should be more movable and spread out through the community so that the whole Bay Area would feel its benefits. I don't think it should be insular or provincial, just San Francisco alone. Other communities in Northern California should participate. and not just by supplying tourists to San Francisco. A Northern California fair would benefit a broader region.

> *The fact that this Fair was going to vanish, and you knew it at the time, that this was only to last one summer, perhaps two, gave it a poignancy and an importance.*

There were a number of reasons why I wanted to write about the Fair. First, I discerned interest in it among other people. The physical remains of the Exposition were almost immediately gone. It had just vanished. That left a sense of loss for the many people who loved it. I thought that readers would find it fun, as I would, to look back on it.

And then, too, the Fair represented a turning point for the State and for the West, as well as for me. It was the last product of the '30s, in a sense. It was a bootstrap operation, like so much in that era — a time of economic depression, social unrest and unhappiness, culminating in something very positive, attractive, and optimistic. All of that was swept away by the war, like my own childhood.

Designers

Air Transportation Building:
Carlo Taliabue, sculptor.

Alameda-Contra Costa Building:
Irvine F. Morrow, architect.
Harry W. Shepherd, landscape architect.

Arch of the Winds:
Lewis P. Hobart, architect.
Hugo Ballin, muralist.

Chief of the Bureau of Horticulture:
Julius L. Girod.

Chief of the Division of Electricity:
George E. Garthrone.

Chinese Village:
Mark Daniels, architect and landscape designer.

Court of Flowers:
Lewis P. Hobart, architect.
Fountain of Life: Olof C. Malmquist, sculptor.
Rainbow statue: Olof C. Malmquist, sculptor.

Court of Honor:
Arthur Brown, Jr., architect.
St. Francis: Clara Huntington, sculptor.

Court of the Moon and Stars:
George W. Kelham and J.H. Clark, architects.
Evening Star: Ettore Cadorin, sculptor.

Court of the Nation:
San Francisco Building and California Building: Timothy L. Pflueger and Clarence A. Tantau, architects.
Federal Building: Timothy L. Pflueger, architect.
Federal Building murals "Conquest of the West by Land and by Water": Herman Voltz, designer. Painted by Herman Voltz and by artists of the Federal Art Project.

Court of Pacifica:
Timothy L. Pflueger, architect.
Pacifica: Ralph Stackpole, sculptor.
The Peacemakers: Esther, Helen, and Margaret Bruton, muralists.
Fountain of the Western Waters: Adaline Kent, Carl George, Sargent Johnson, Brents Carlton, Jacques Schnier, Ruth Cravath Wakefield, Cecilia B. Braham, and Helen Phillips, sculptors.

Court of Reflections:
Lewis P. Hobart, architect.
Penguin Girl: Edgar Walter, sculptor.

Court of the Seven Seas:
George W. Kelham, and J.H. Clark, architects.
Sixteen galleon prows tipped with the winged Spirit of Adventure: P.O. Tognelli, sculptor.
Discovery, Christopher Columbus: P.O. Tognelli, sculptor.
Creation: Haig Patigian, sculptor.

Deputy Chief of the Bureau of Horticulture:
Elmer G. Gould.

Director of Color:
Jessie E. Stanton.

Director of Illumination:
A.F. Dickerson.

Fine Arts Palace:
George W. Kelham, architect.
Edward L. Frick, architect of facade.

GGIE Architectural Commission:
George W. Kelham
Arthur Brown, Jr.
Lewis P. Hobart
William G. Merchant
Timothy L. Pflueger
Ernest E. Weihe
W.P. Day.

Hall of Flowers:
Mark Daniels, landscape architect.

Hall of Western States Auditorium:
Salici's Puppets Panel: Robert B. Howard, painter, sculptor.

Japanese Pavilion:
Yoshizo Utida and Tatunae Toki, architects.
Takeshi Tamura and Nagao Sakurai, landscape architects.

Magic Carpet:
Julius L. Girod, horticulturist.

Mission Trails Building:
Harold A. Edmondson and Robert Stanton, architects.

Norway Pavilion:
Magnus Poulson, architect.

Pacific House:
William G. Merchant, architect.

Pavilion of the Philippines:
Gregorio P. Gutierrez, architect.

Portals of the Pacific:
Ernest E. Weihe, architect.
Elephants and Howdaws: Donald Macky, sculptor.

Redwood Empire Building:
William G. Merchant and Bernard R. Maybeck, architects.

South Tower:
George W. Kelham, architect.
P.O. Tognelli, sculptor.

Temple Compound:
William G. Merchant, architect.

Temples of the East:
Bernard R. Maybeck and William G. Merchant, architects.
Ocean Breeze: Jacques Schnier, sculptor.

Tower of the Sun:
Arthur Brown, Jr., architect.
Phoenix: Olof C. Malmquist, sculptor.

Treasure Garden:
George W. Kelham and J.H. Clark, architects.

Yerba Buena Clubhouse:
William W. Wurster, architect.
Garden figure: Haig Patigian, sculptor.

Index

156